Th *500 Hidden Secrets of*

BANGKOK

INTRODUCTION

Bangkok is Asia's most captivating city. A melange of the old and the new, it gives the traveller everything, from atmospheric crumbling colonial mansions and Chinese shophouses set alongside canals, to snazzy new rooftop Michelin-chef run restaurants that overlook one of the world's greatest conglomerations of neon lit skyscrapers and pulsing streets.

The city is full of contradictions. It is the only capital in Southeast Asia never to be colonised, yet also home to more 7-11 convenience stores than you'll find in your home country. Tuk tuks and Mercedes compete for space on the gridlocked roads, yet longtail boats and river ferries deliver you to communities built on wooden stilts, where you'll find traditional Thai puppetry and other age-old cultural traditions still flourishing.

This book will assist you in discovering all sides of Bangkok, from finding the 5 best places to dine along the river to uncovering the city's 5 best shrines or 5 best old colonial buildings, or the latest speakeasies for a great cocktail. It is an intimate guide to all that Bangkok has to offer, both off the beaten track as well as to the most trending and happening places. Up to date and well researched by the author, a 15-year resident, you'll discover the best walks around town, and even find the 5 best places for ice cream – which is actually something pretty vital, given the hot and sticky tropical weather that graces the city much of the year.

HOW TO USE
THIS BOOK?

This guide lists 500 things you need to know about Bangkok in 100 different categories. Most of these are places to visit, with practical information to help you find your way. Others are bits of information that help you get to know the city and its habitants. The aim of this guide is to inspire, not to cover the city from A to Z.

The places listed in the guide are given an address, including the neighbourhood (for example Pathumwan or Sukhumvit), and a number. The neighbourhood and number allow you to find the locations on the maps at the beginning of the book: first look for the map of the corresponding neighbourhood, then look for the right number. A word of caution however: these maps are not detailed enough to allow you to find specific locations in the city. You can obtain an excellent map from any tourist office or in most hotels. Or the addresses can be located on a smartphone.

Please also bear in mind that cities change all the time. The chef who hits a high note one day may be uninspiring on the day you happen to visit. The hotel ecstatically reviewed in this book might suddenly go downhill under a new manager. The bar considered one of the 5 bars that rock might be empty on the night you visit. This is obviously a highly personal selection. You might not always agree with it. If you want to leave a comment, recommend a bar or reveal your favourite secret place, please visit the website *www.the500hiddensecrets.com* – you'll also find free tips and the latest news about the series there – or follow *@500hiddensecrets* on Instagram or Facebook and leave a comment.

THE AUTHOR

Dave Stamboulis is a Greek-American who has called Bangkok home for the past 15 years. A professional photographer and travel writer, he is an avid globetrotter, mountain trekker, and is noted for his award-winning book, *Odysseus' Last Stand*, detailing his seven-year and 45.000-kilometre bicycle ride around the world.

A lover of craft beer, well-mixed cocktails, and ethnic cuisine, Dave can be found checking out the latest rooftop bars and speakeasies that seem to spring up by the day in Bangkok, looking for the most authentic hole-in-the-wall street eateries, or finding hidden gems like Bang Krachao, Bangkok's 'lung' and largest green space, where the average visitor, or even resident, doesn't get to.

Dave hopes that this guidebook will enable visitors to explore the less visited and more atmospheric sides of Bangkok, the old neighbourhoods that are slowly disappearing, where the slow-paced and easy going Thai friendliness is still on display, and the big modern metropolis is still held at bay.

In making this Luster guide a reality, Dave owes a debt of gratitude to his partner, Raquel Mogado, for helping with photo choices and guidance, going on long explorations throughout the bowels of the city to get the latest information, and putting up with endless evenings spent slaving over the computer. Also, a big thanks goes out to his editor, Dettie Luyten, who made the writing and proofing process as smooth and easy as could be possible.

BANGKOK

overview

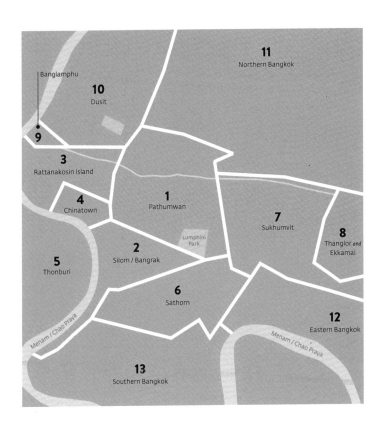

11 Northern Bangkok

Banglamphu

10 Dusit

9

3 Rattanakosin Island

4 Chinatown

1 Pathumwan

7 Sukhumvit

8 Thanglor *and* Ekkamai

Lumphini Park

2 Silom / Bangrak

5 Thonburi

6 Sathorn

12 Eastern Bangkok

Menam / Chao Praya

Menam / Chao Praya

13 Southern Bangkok

Map 1
PATHUMWAN

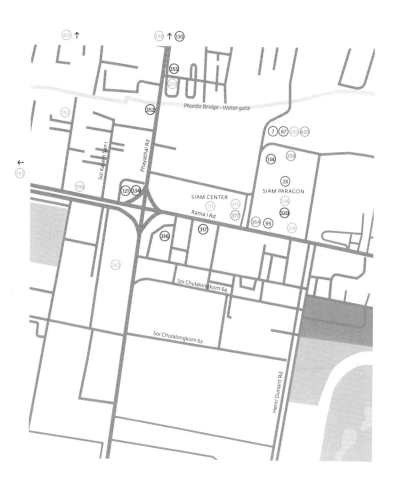

Map 2
SILOM / BANG RAK

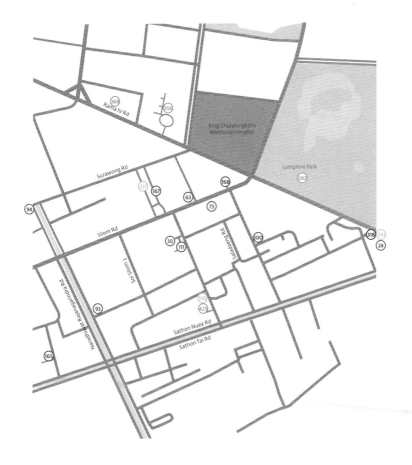

King Chulalongkorn Memorial Hospital

Lumphini Park

Rama IV Rd

Surawong Rd

Silom Rd

Sathon Nuea Rd

Sathon Tai Rd

Soi Silom 3

Naradhiwat Rajanagarindra Rd

Saladaeng Rd

Map 3

RATTANAKOSIN
ISLAND

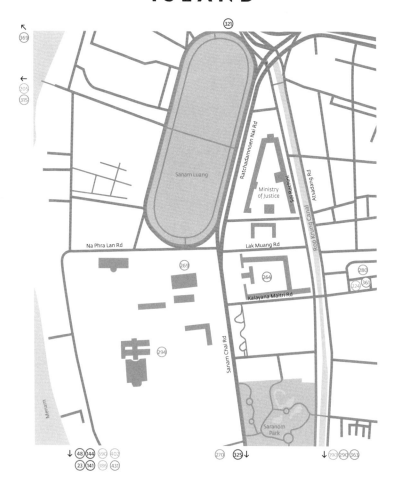

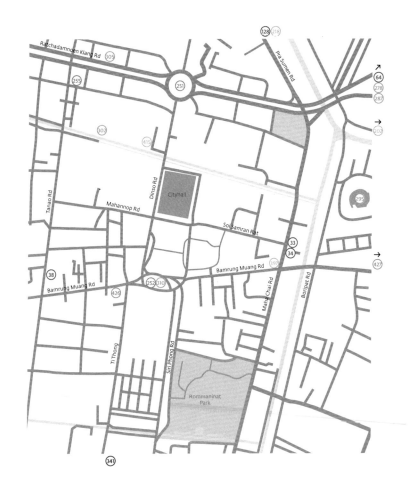

Map 4
CHINATOWN

Map 5
THONBURI

Map 6
SATHORN

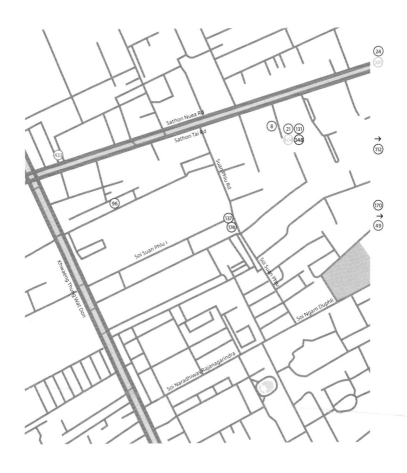

Sathon Nuea Rd
Sathon Tai Rd
Suan Phlu Rd
Soi Suan Phlu 1
Khwaeng Thung Wat Don
Soi Suan Phlu
Soi Ngam Duphli
Soi Naradhiwas Rajanagarindra

(24)
(391)
(8) (21) (131)
(404)(348)
→
(112)
(170)
→
(49)
(433)
(96)
(137)
(174)

Map 7
SUKHUMVIT

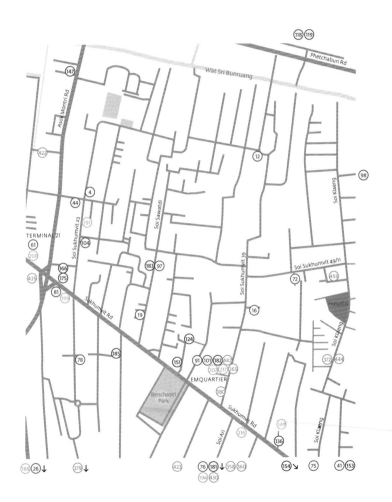

Map 8
THONGLOR / EKKAMAI

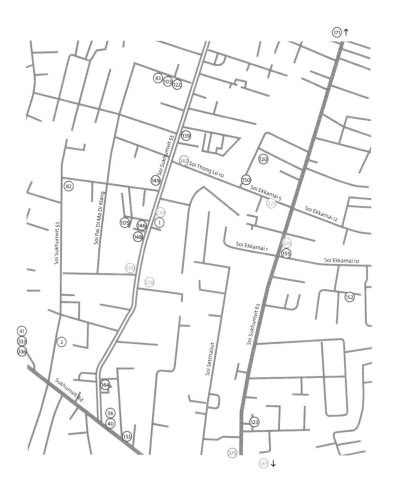

Map 9
BANGLAMPHU

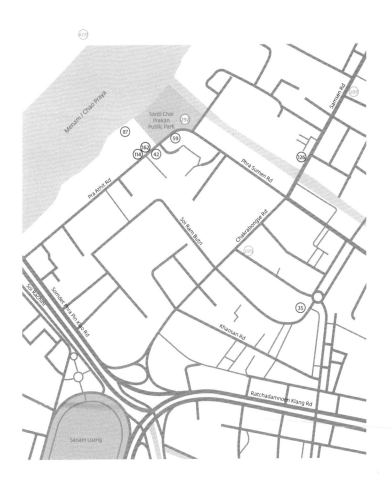

Map 10
DUSIT

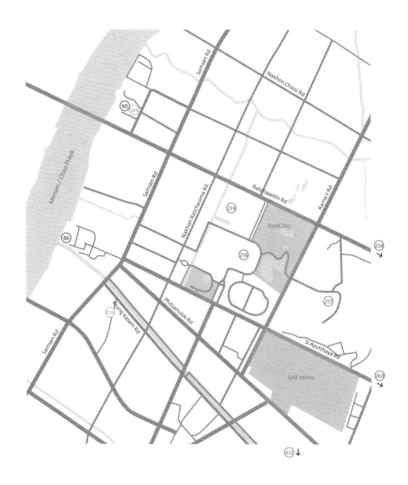

Map 11

NORTHERN

BANGKOK

Map 12
EASTERN
BANGKOK

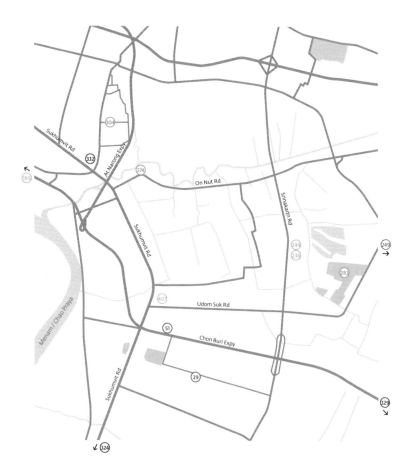

Map 13
SOUTHERN
BANGKOK

CRAB AND CLAW

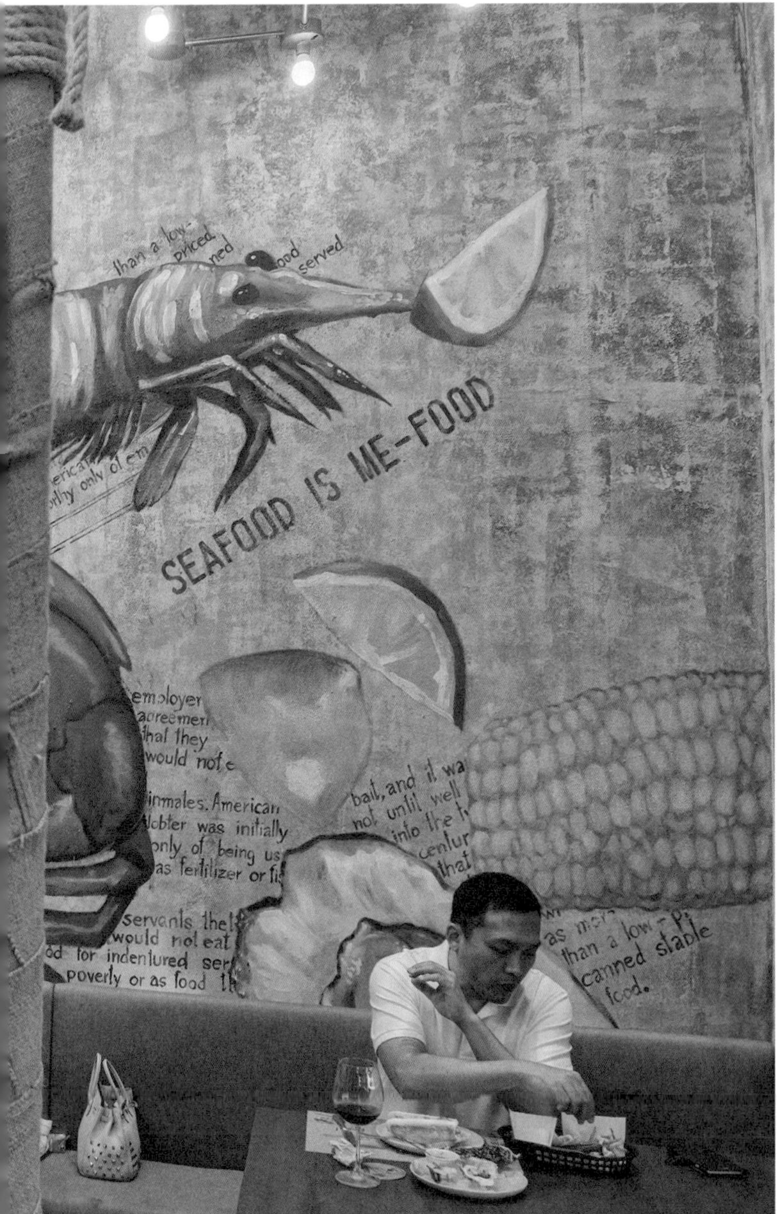
SEAFOOD IS ME-FOOD

110 PLACES TO EAT OR BUY GOOD FOOD

The 5 best
THAI
restaurants

---

1 SUPANNIGA EATING ROOM

160/11 Sukhumvit Soi 55
Thonglor/Ekkamai ⑧
+66 (0)2 714 7508
*www.supanniga
eatingroom.com*

This simple shophouse eatery serves up traditional dishes from the owner's family cookbook, mainly his grandmother's recipes from Thailand's eastern seaboard. Dishes like *moo chamuang*, a succulent pork stew made with medicinal *chamuang* (garcinia) leaves represent the unique menu, which features hearty, real Thai dishes that you'll be hard pressed to find elsewhere in Bangkok.

2 BO.LAN

24 Sukhumvit Soi 53
Thonglor/Ekkamai ⑧
+66 (0)2 260 2962
www.bolan.co.th

Duangporn 'Bo' Songvisava and her chef husband Dylan Jones, both of whom cooked for Nahm, David Thompson's Thai restaurant in London, run this amazing place which is focused on becoming Thailand's first zero carbon footprint restaurant. Songvisava was awarded Best Female Chef in Asia in 2013, and Bo.lan focuses on authentic fine Thai dining made with organic and locally sourced high-end ingredients.

3 BAAN SOMTUM

9/1 Soi Srivieng
(off Sathorn Road)
Sathorn ⑥
+66 (0)2 630 3486
www.baansomtum.com

The food here says it all. Focusing mainly on Isaan (northeastern) Thai treats like *sai krok* stuffed spicy sausage or *kor moo yang* grilled pork shoulder, Baan Somtum churns out plate upon plate of consistently delicious treats.

4 THE LOCAL

32 Sukhumvit Soi 23
Sukhumvit ⑦
+66 (0)2 664 0664
*www.thelocal
thaicuisine.com*

Housed in a beautiful 70-year-old traditional Thai teak wood home, The Local specialises in serving hard to find dishes from all over Thailand. Owner Can Markawat comes from a family of foodies who have run successful restaurants for decades. Even your Thai friends will be impressed.

5 PASTE

AT: GAYSORN VILLAGE,
3RD FLOOR
999 Ploenchit Road
Pathumwan ①
+66 (0)2 656 1003
www.pastebangkok.com

Australian chef Jason Bailey and his Thai partner, chef Bee Satongun, take authentic and royal palace Thai recipes and balance them beautifully, merging authentic Thai dining flavours with innovative fine dining. Be prepared for a real feast.

5 places to
SPLURGE ON DINNER

---

6 GAGGAN

68/1 Soi Langsuan
Pathumwan ①
+66 (0)2 652 1700
www.eatgaggan.com

Winner of the prestigious San Pellegrino Best Restaurant in Asia award in 2015, 2016, and 2017, Gaggan takes Indian food and turns it on its head, combining molecular techniques and progressive interpretations to create a stunning dining experience. The 19-part tasting menu is worth every pocket-draining baht for the experience.

7 SRA BUA

AT: SIAM KEMPINSKI HOTEL
991/9 Rama I Road
Pathumwan ①
+66 (0)2 162 9000
*www.kempinski
bangkok.com*

Tom yum served as a powder, *pad thai* served as a paste? You might not recognise any of the dishes served here, but your taste buds will certainly appreciate them. Sra Bua gives molecular twists to Thai favourites and is almost as much a magic show as it is a unique knockout fine dining experience.

8 NAHM

AT: THE METROPOLITAN HOTEL
27 South Sathorn Road
Sathorn ⑥
+66 (0)2 625 3388
*www.comohotels.com/
metropolitanbangkok/
dining/nahm*

Michelin-starred chef David Thompson is recognised as one of the world's premier Thai food masters, and the authentic recipes here are cranked up to Thai spice levels, so you needn't worry about Thompson not being Thai. Nahm is one of Bangkok's top food experiences.

9 LE NORMANDIE

AT: MANDARIN ORIENTAL HOTEL
48 Oriental Avenue
Silom/Bang Rak ②
+66 (0)2 659 9000
www.mandarinoriental.
com/bangkok/fine-dining/
le-normandie

You wouldn't expect to eat foie gras with roast Sisteron rack of lamb in Bangkok, but Le Normandie combines both true haute French cuisine with dazzling views of the Chao Phraya River. Located in Bangkok's Grande Dame, the Mandarin Oriental Hotel, it's classy, romantic and pricey.

10 L'ATELIER DE JOEL ROBUCHON

AT: MAHANAKHON CUBE,
5TH FLOOR
96 Naradhiwas
Rajanagarindra Road
Sathorn ⑥
+66 (0)2 001 0698
www.robuchon-
bangkok.com

While Monsieur Robuchon, the world's most decorated Michelin chef, isn't actually here, his protégé Olivier Limousin, who ran Robuchon's London and Paris branches, getting two Michelin stars for each, actually is. Here, he performs for guests at an interactive counter. It's intimate, very expensive, and a foodie nirvana.

10 L'ATELIER DE JOEL ROBUCHON

5 authentic
CHINESE
restaurants

---

11 THE CHINA HOUSE
AT: MANDARIN ORIENTAL
48 Oriental Avenue
Silom/Bang Rak ②
+66 (0)2 659 9000
www.mandarin
oriental.com

Decorated like Shanghai in the Roaring Twenties, the Mandarin Oriental's China House serves the best Peking duck in town along with an unlimited dim sum buffet during the week and a delicious weekend brunch. It's Bangkok's classiest Chinese option.

12 HONG BAO
104 Sukhumvit Soi 39
Sukhumvit ⑦
+66 (0)2 662 3565
www.hongbao
restaurant.com

Dim sum lovers can rejoice, as Hong Bao serves its array of staples all day long. Choose from *har gau* shrimp dumplings to grilled pork rib bites. The dim sum of-ferings here are some of the most diverse and popular in the city. This branch, along with another at Central Embassy, is the easiest to access.

13 MAN HO
AT: JW MARRIOTT HOTEL
4 Sukhumvit Soi 2
Pathumwan ⑦
+66 (0)2 656 7700
www.jwmarriott
bangkok.com

An all-you-can-eat dim sum buffet draws crowds here, and favourites like abalone soup and Peking duck served in the refined environment of the JW Marriott Hotel makes Man Ho an excellent choice if you are looking for fine Chinese dining.

14 DIN TAI FUNG
AT: CENTRALWORLD,
7TH FLOOR
**99/9 Rama I Road
Pathumwan** ①
+66 (0)2 646 1282

Din Tai Fung has been named one of the world's ten best restaurants, as well as having been awarded a Michelin star, and the Bangkok branches of the Taiwanese dumpling masters don't disappoint either. The *xiaolongbao* soup dumplings are exquisitely crafted with 18 folds, and are filled with succulent pork broth that just explodes when you bite into them.

15 MEI JIANG
AT: THE PENINSULA HOTEL
**333 Charoennakorn
Road
Thonburi** ⑤
+66 (0)2 020 2888
*www.bangkok.
peninsula.com*

The elegant Peninsula Hotel's signature restaurant combines traditional Chinese with innovative creations. Sample marinated roasted pigeon while looking out on the hotel's lush gardens and the Chao Phraya River. It's worth the trip across to the Thonburi side just for the atmosphere alone.

14 DIN TAI FUNG

The 5 best

JAPANESE

restaurants

---

16 **BANKARA RAMEN**
AT: THE MANOR
32/1 Sukhumvit Soi 39
Sukhumvit ⑦
+66 (0)2 662 5162
www.ramen-bankara.com

Bankara takes ramen to new heights. The *tonkatsu* stewed pork belly is on almost every diner's table, and the authentic thick and huge bowls of noodles are perfectly replicated from their legendary Ikebukuro branch in Tokyo. The queue at the door attests to just how popular they are on the Bangkok ramen scene as well.

17 **GINZA SUSHI ISHI**
AT: ERAWAN BANGKOK HOTEL, LG/F
494 Phloenchit Road
Pathumwan ①
+66 (0)2 250 0014
www.ginza-sushiichi.jp

With limited seating (11 seats) reservations are a must here, as is a deep pocketbook for investing in Ginza's *omakase* chef's tasting menu, which costs 4000 baht. You are guaranteed some superb *sashimi* though, served by chefs trained by Michelin master Masakazu Ishibashi, plus the freshest fish in town.

18 **ZUMA**
AT: ST. REGIS HOTEL
159 Rajadamri Road
Pathumwan ①
+66 (0)2 252 4707
www.zumarestaurant.com

Zuma takes traditional Japanese *izakaya* food and gives it a sophisticated twist, serving up some of the city's most well prepared and innovative Japanese cuisine. Gourmet food aside, don't miss their signature rhubarb martini, which blends rhubarb infused sake with -42° chilled vodka.

19 ISAO

5 Sukhumvit Soi 31
Sukhumvit ⑦
+66 (0)2 258 0645
www.isaotaste.com

Isao is one of the few restaurants in Bangkok with a line outside 365 nights a year, and the wait is well justified. The owner did a stint at Green Tea, the famed Chicago creative sushi eatery, and it reflects in the amazing concoctions here, like the Jackie, a caterpillar shaped sushi roll with shrimp, roe, and tempura.

20 MORIMOTO BANGKOK

AT: MAHANAKHON CUBE,
4TH FLOOR
96 Naradhiwas
Rajanagarindra Road
Sathorn ⑥
+66 (0)2 060 9099
*www.morimoto
bangkok.com*

Television culinary superstar Iron Chef Masaharu Morimoto has brought his talented act to Bangkok, combining traditional *kaiseki* Japanese cuisine with international fusion, the result of which is a blend of delectable fare. Think *hamachi* tacos served alongside the freshest *sashimi* cuts.

18 ZUMA

5 restaurants with an
UNFORGETTABLE VIEW

---

21 **VERTIGO**
AT: BANYAN TREE HOTEL
21/100 South Sathorn Road
Sathorn ⑥
+66 (0)2 679 1200
www.banyantree.com

This is possibly Bangkok's most staggering panorama, perched closer to the clouds than the streets below. Located on the roof of the Banyan Tree Hotel, Vertigo gives 360° views all around, and every table has a real bird's-eye view. It is also wildly expensive.

22 **SIROCCO**
AT: LEBUA STATE TOWER
1055 Silom Road
Silom/Bang Rak ②
+66 (0)2 624 9555
www.lebua.com/sirocco

Sirocco overlooks the entire sweep of the Chao Phraya River, with tables set out on a large deck looking back at all the neon of the Bangkok night. While the Lebua is home to several sky high restaurants and bars, this one takes the cake due to being out in the open.

23 **THE DECK**
36-38 Soi Pratoo Nok Yoong, Maharat Road
Rattanakosin Island ③
+66 (0)2 221 9158
www.arunresidence.com

While most view restaurants in Bangkok are all about height, The Deck goes for low elevation and a great river and temple view of Wat Arun. The restaurant hugs the Chao Phraya River and looks directly across at the temple. Come at sunset and then watch the temple get illuminated as the lights go on.

22 SIROCCO

25 SCARLETT

24 PARK SOCIETY

AT: SO SOFITEL BANGKOK
2 North Sathorn Road
Sathorn ⑥ ②
+66 (0)2 624 0000
www.so-sofitel-bangkok.
com/wine-dine/park-
society

Not only can you enjoy foie gras, you can do so to the city's best view of its largest urban green space, Lumphini Park, below. There is a monthly degustation menu and also a selection of shareable tapas plates that can be enjoyed with drinks on the terrace overlooking the green, backed by the lit cityscape behind it.

25 SCARLETT

AT: PULLMAN G HOTEL,
37TH FLOOR
188 Silom Road
Silom/Bang Rak ②
+66 (0)96 860 7990

Scarlett provides French bistro cuisine with a 37th floor view of the Chao Phraya River and the cityscape of the Central Business District. You can choose between an outdoor terrace or the cosy interior to take in all the night lights. The huge wine cellar, fine meats, and superlative views make for one superb combo.

The 5 best international
FOOD STORES

---

26 **EL MERCADO**
490 Soi Phai Sing To,
Klong Toei
Sukhumvit ⑦
+66 (0)2 258 1385
www.elmercado
bangkok.com

The European owners here got their inspiration from Rungis in Paris and La Boqueria in Barcelona, as you can select your own cheese and meat platters, get a baguette and bottle of wine, and eat right on the premises. El Mercado is a deli, a restaurant and a market all in one.

27 **TOPS GOURMET MARKET**
AT: CENTRAL CHIDLOM
1027 Ploenchit Road
Pathumwan ①
+66 (0)2 655 7648
www.centralfoodhall.com/
en/store

Don't come here with a full wallet, as it will be empty when you leave. The array of imported food items, top local produce and fruit is staggering. The cheese shop could compete with any French fromagerie, and the sushi, seafood, and roasted meats sections are equally as inspiring.

28 GOURMET MARKET

AT: SIAM PARAGON G/F
**991/1 Rama I Road
Pathumwan ①**
+66 (0)2 690 1000
*www.gourmetmarket
thailand.com*

Wilh one of widest selections of items
from around the world, chances are – if
it can to be found in Bangkok – you'll get
it here. There is a section of imported
Japanese foods, a huge wine cellar, the
freshest seafood in town, and the added
bonus of the mall's food court being right
outside if you're hungry.

29 SLOANE'S

**640 Soi La Salle (betw 34
and 36), Sukhumvit 105
Eastern Bangkok ⑬**
+66 (0)2 398 2294
www.sloanes.co.th

Butcher Joe Sloane creates artisanal meat
products using fine ingredients from ethical
farming practices. From pâté to sausages
made from natural casings, cured and
barbecued items, everything here is top
notch. Virtually every high end restaurant
in town gets their meat from his personal
deli, so you'll be in good company.

30 GARGANTUA BOUCHERIE

**10/5 Soi Convent
Silom/Bang Rak ②**
+66 (0)2 630 4577

The owner here is a fifth generation
French butcher and his carne knowledge
is unbeatable. He cuts his meat according
to the rules stipulated by French
butchery, and sources cuts from local
beef like Charolais cattle from Thailand's
northeast, ensuring import quality meat
without the extravagant import prices.

The 5 tastiest places for
STREET FOOD

---

31 **KHAO RAT GAENG JEK PUI**
Cnr. of Mangkon Road and Charoen Krung Road
Chinatown ④
+66 (0)2 222 5229

Khao rat gaeng means 'curry over rice', and at places like this you can choose several curry toppings to go over a plate of jasmine rice. This stall is also known as 'musical chairs rice curry', due to the fact that there are no tables, only stools, which immediately get taken over by another diner the minute one gets up!

32 **JOK PRINCE**
1391 Charoen Krung Road
Silom/Bang Rak ②
+66 (0)81 916 4390

Jok, or rice congee, is a popular street meal, and Jok Prince differentiates itself from the others by giving its rice porridge a smoky flavour by slightly burning the rice that is on the bottom of the pan. It is said to be a great cure for a hangover.

33 **PAD THAI THIP SAMAI**
313-315 Mahachai Road
Rattanakosin Island ③
+66 (0)2 221 6280

Just watching the assembly line factory-style precision here makes it worth coming. Huge woks are used to stir fry massive batches of what is claimed to be the city's best *pad thai*, with jumbo shrimp and thin egg wrapping sealing the deal. The line outside is often down the block.

34 JAE FAI

31 KHAO RAT GAENG JEK PUI

34 JAE FAI

327 Mahachai Road
Rattanakosin Island ③
+66 (0)2 223 9384

Come watch the Mercedes roll up to eat Bangkok's most expensive street food. An old auntie still presides over the stove here, cooking up *pad kee mao* 'drunkard's noodles', which normally cost 30 baht elsewhere, but go for over 300 here. Jae Fai has become legendary ever since N.Y. Times food critic Bob Halliday raved about it over a decade ago.

35 AISA ROT DEE

178 Tani Road
Banglamphu ⑨
+66 (0)2 282 6378

It's just around the corner from Khao San Road, yet few tourists find this gem, tucked into a somewhat hidden courtyard. The highlight here is the *khao mok gai* chicken biryani, served with a delicious mint sauce, and there are other dishes from the Thai-Muslim tradition to choose from as well.

5
THAI DISHES
you shouldn't miss

---

36 **SOM TAM**
AT: BAAN SOMTUM
**9/1 Soi Srivieng (off
Sathorn Road)
Sathorn** ⑥
+66 (0)2 630 3486
www.baansomtum.com

Perhaps Thailand's most beloved go-to dish, *som tam* is spicy papaya salad, made with gratings from the green papaya, mixed up in a mortar with chilies, peanuts, lime juice, and palm sugar. Some versions throw in crab, mango, and even fermented fish paste. Try it in many variations at Baan Somtum.

37 **KHAO MAN GAI**
AT: GO ANG PRATUNAM
**966 Petchaburi Road
(at Soi 30)
Pathumwan** ①
+66 (0)2 252 6325

Also known as Hainanese chicken rice, this is a Chinese immigrant dish that features boiled chicken served over rice. What makes it special is the accompanying soy sauce, garlic, vinegar, and chili sauce, put over the chicken and making it burst with flavour. Try it at perennial favourite Go Ang Pratunam.

38 **KHAO NIAOW MAMUANG**
AT: KOR PANICH
**431-433 Tanao Road
Rattanakosin Island** ③
+66 (0)2 221 3554

Technically a dessert, but it's so heavy and filling you can eat it as a meal. This dish combines fresh mango served over sticky (glutinous) rice, topped with sweetened coconut milk. Eat the best in town at Kor Panich, which has been in business for almost a century.

39 **LARB**
AT: LUNG YAI
532 Din Daeng Road
Northern Bangkok ⑪
+66 (0)2 642 4084

Larb is a meat 'salad' that originated in Thailand's northeast. Pork is the most popular, but it is also made with chicken, beef, and there are excellent versions that use duck and catfish. The cooked meat gets pounded in a mortar along with plenty of chilies, shallots, lime juice, and Thai herbs. Try an array of excellent *larbs* at Lung Yai.

40 **TOM YUM**
AT: 55 POCHANA
1087-91 Sukhumvit
Road (at Thonglor
intersection)
Thonglor/Ekkamai ⑧
+66 (0)2 391 2021

Tom yum is typically a spicy and sour soup made with lemongrass, *galanga* Thai ginger, *kaffir* lime leaves, fish sauce, and chilies. Try the variations on the soup while here, as they have totally different tastes. *Nam khon* adds cream or coconut milk to the broth, whereas *potek* offers a clear and more pungent broth. Try them at 55 Pochana.

The 5 best places for
BURGERS

---

41   CRYING THAIGER

27/1 Sukhumvit Soi 51
Sukhumvit ⑦⑧
+66 (0)97 052 8861
www.thaigerbkk.com

Daniel Thaiger, named after the American owner and his Thai wife's son, was Bangkok's first food truck, with lines down the block each evening queuing up for his meaty hamburgers. Thaiger has since moved on to bigger things, opening up a real restaurant in trendy Thonglor, and serving up Mediterranean lamb burgers, truffle fries, and other gourmet eats.

42   ESCAPADES

112 Phra Athit Road
Banglamphu ⑨
+66 (0)81 406 3773

Looking more like a garage than a restaurant, Escapades serves up some of Bangkok's finest burgers. The diner was started by a Cordon Bleu chef, and the lamb burgers on charcoal buns or two-patty Angus beef burgers with truffle sauce are served with unbeatable milkshakes.

43   FIREHOUSE

33/25-26 Sukhumvit
Soi 11
Sukhumvit ⑦
+66 (0)2 651 3643

Firehouse has American pub grub down to a fine art, with organic beef burgers and veggie burgers fronting a large choice menu. The place is decked out with firehouse bric-à-brac, and while the burgers aren't quite as highbrow as some others listed here, neither are the prices.

44 **CHEF BAR**
21 Sukhumvit Soi 2
Sukhumvit ⑦
+66 (0)80 052 7336

The burgers here will overwhelm you, with creations like smoked beef, almond pesto, and gorgonzola leading the burger charge. Chef Roland holds court in this tiny shophouse, with room for only about 10 people inside, and there is a daily changing selection of dishes other than just classic burgers to keep everyone satisfied.

45 **25 DEGREES**
AT: PULLMAN G HOTEL
188 Silom Road
Silom/Bang Rak ②
+66 (0)2 238 1991

Named after the temperature difference between raw and well done, this 24-hour dining venue resembles a glitzy American diner, with red stools, marble flooring, and a choice of burgers that allows you to either build your own or go for their superb signature ones, all of which use imported U.S. beef.

45 25 DEGREES

The 5 most
ROMANTIC
restaurants

---

46 **L'APPART**
AT: SOFITEL SUKHUMVIT
189 Sukhumvit Road
Sukhumvit ⑦
+66 (0)2 126 9999
www.sofitel-bangkok-
sukhumvit.com

L'Appart resembles a 19th-century Parisien apartment, with intimate nooks complete with sunken sofas and copies of French classics set on the side tables. Combine the ambience with the haute cuisine French fare, plus a bottle of fine wine or champagne, and you and your date have the amorous night of the year all set up.

47 **MEZZALUNA**
AT: LEBUA STATE TOWER
1055 Silom Road
Silom/Bang Rak ②
+66 (0)2 624 9555
www.lebua.com/
mezzaluna

At Mezzaluna, you overlook the sweep of the Chao Phraya River with a 180° panorama across Bangkok. Perched up on the 65th floor of the Lebua State Tower, not only are the vistas jaw dropping, but the innovative chef tasting menu will have you in awe.

48 **SALA RATTANAKOSIN EATERY AND BAR**
AT: SALA RATTANAKOSIN
39 Maharat Road
Rattanakosin Island ③
+66 (0)2 622 1388
www.salarattanakosin.com

Reserve yourself a front table here, facing out at the Chao Phraya River and Wat Arun, which sits directly across from you. Sunsets, blue hour, and the temple lights coming on make for an amorous setting, and the superb fine dining options seal the deal.

49 ISSAYA SIAMESE

4 Soi Sri Aksorn,
Chua Ploeng Road
Sathorn ⑥
+66 (0)2 672 9040
www.issaya.com

Set in a lovely century-old Thai mansion, Issaya has won local accolades for outstanding Thai food made from farm fresh ingredients and was named one of Asia's top 50 restaurants in 2016 by San Pellegrino. The setting is hopelessly romantic, either inside the intimate mansion, or lounging on the beanbag chairs on the front lawn.

50 SUPANNIGA CRUISE

Boat departs from River
City Pier 2
23 Trok Rongnam-
khaeng, Yota Road
Chinatown ②
+66 (0)2 714 7608
www.supannigacruise.com

Why settle for looking at the river when you can be on it? The foodie owner of Supanniga Eating Room now has a boat restaurant as well. There are just 4 to 5 tables on each deck, where diners are served gourmet Thai meals and champagne while languidly navigating the Chao Phraya.

50 SUPANNIGA CRUISE

The 5
QUIRKIEST
restaurants

---

51 **KRATON FLYING CHICKEN**
99/1 Bang Na-Trat Road
(opposite BITEC)
Eastern Bangkok ⑫
+66 (0)2 399 5202

At Kraton, your grilled chicken does not cross the road to get to the other side, but instead is set in a catapult, and then vaulted across the restaurant to a waiter who is riding a unicycle and wearing a helmet affixed with a trio of metal skewers! The waiters catch the birds on the fly, and then pedal them up to your table!

52 **HAJIME ROBOT**
AT: MONOPOLY PARK,
3RD FLOOR
59/27 Rama III Road
Southern Bangkok ⑬
+66 (0)2 683 1670
www.hajimerobot.com

The *yakiniku* and *shabu shabu* buffet is reason enough to come here for a pig-out, but what makes Hajime stand out is the use of samurai-dressed robots which dance and then deliver food along a track to your table. Yeah, it's a gimmick to draw in clients, but the kids will love it.

53 **DINE IN THE DARK**
AT: SHERATON GRANDE
250 Sukhumvit Road
Sukhumvit ⑦
+66 (0)2 649 8358
*www.dineinthedark
bangkok.com*

Your visually impaired or blind waitress will lead you into a pitch black room (no cell phones or watch lights allowed), and you'll proceed to be served a four-course dinner, all of which you will have to rely on taste and smell as to identify what it is.

54 CABBAGES AND CONDOMS

10 Sukhumvit Soi 12
Sukhumvit ⑦
+66 (0)2 229 4610
www.cabbages
andcondoms.net

Cabbages and Condoms has won awards for its commitment to safe sex and sexual health, donating part of your bill to community projects. The vast menu has a range of Thai favourites. There are condom-themed characters placed throughout the restaurant, and the motto of the owners is 'our food won't get you pregnant'.

55 FAIKEAW YAOWARAT

Yaowarat Soi 11
Chinatown ④
+66 (0)97 232 8553

It's worth coming to Chinatown just to witness the chef here perform at this street eatery. Every ten minutes, he stir-fries a bunch of morning glory, known for its flame inducement when sautéed in a wok full of hot oil, producing pyromaniac-worthy fireworks, and plenty of gasps from the audience.

55 FAIKEAW YAOWARAT

The 5 best
HOLE-IN-THE-WALL EATERIES

---

56 **55 POCHANA**
1087-1091 Sukhumvit Road (at Thonglor intersection)
Thonglor/Ekkamai ⑧
+66 (0)2 391 2021

55 Pochana is an institution. It has been around for decades, even had a song written about it by a Thai band, and despite slightly modernising, still serves up delicious food at rock bottom prices. Note that every table has the *or suan* oyster and egg sizzling hot plate on it, as well as a bowl of what might be Bangkok's best *tom yum*.

57 **NAI MONG HOI TOD**
539 Phlap Phla Chai Road
Chinatown ④
+66 (0)89 773 3133

Few visitors to Bangkok know *hoi tod*, a dish similar to *pad thai* made with fried mussels, oysters, and eggs. This dive restaurant sees foodies making the pilgrimage to taste perhaps the best in town, with a choice of crispy and super crispy oysters and mussels coming off the grill, served up with a sweet chili dipping sauce.

58 **PRACHAK**
1415 Charoen Krung Road
Silom/Bang Rak ②
+66 (0)2 234 3755

Prachak has been in business since 1897 and it is still hard to find an empty stool here. The old-school Chinese-style eatery specialises in roast duck, served with plum and chili sauce, and is also noted for its crab and shrimp dumplings, which come with noodle soup.

59 ROTI MATABA

**136 Phra Athit Road
Banglamphu ⑨
+66 (0)2 282 2119
*www.roti-mataba.net***

This tiny and packed place is legendary, serving roti and curry to the faithful since 1943. The surrounding neighbourhood has become hip and trendy, but Roti Mataba remains firmly old-school, no-frills, and still dishes out mouthwatering curries or sweet banana rotis if you just want dessert.

60 HOME ISLAMIC CUISINE

**186 Charoen Krung
Soi 36 (across from
the French Embassy)
Silom/Bang Rak ②
+66 (0)2 234 7911**

The owner here was a former goat butcher, and needless to say, he knows his meat. So, it's no surprise that Home Islamic serves up the best *mutton biryani* that you will find in Thailand. The restaurant is hidden down a dead end street by the river, but it is well worth seeking out for its outstanding food.

57 NAI MONG HOI TOD

5 lovely and colourful
FOOD COURTS

---

61 TERMINAL 21
AT: TERMINAL 21 MALL,
5TH FLOOR
88 Sukhumvit Soi 19
Sukhumvit ⑦
+66 (0)2 108 0888
www.terminal21.co.th

Usually, food courts in malls are bland and overpriced versions of the stuff you can get on the street. Terminal 21's food court bucks the trend, with a vast array of vendors and food choices, almost all of which are delicious, and the prices aren't much higher than you'll find out in the heat.

62 OR TOR KOR
101 Kamphaeng Phet
Road, Chatuchak
Northern Bangkok ⑪
+66 (0)2 279 2080
www.ortorkormarket.
com/2013/otk-market

You'll pay a bit extra for your street food here, but the quality is unrivalled. Set in a corner of the market that sells Royal Project produce, where all the restaurants come to buy, the small food court here serves up gourmet versions of all your favourite street selections from every region of Thailand.

**63 THANIYA PLAZA FOOD
COURT**
Soi Thaniya
Silom/Bang Rak ②

Soi Thaniya turns into a seedy Japanese hostess bar street at night, but come here by day, and halfway up the alley you will find a giant array of some of Bangkok's best street food, with dozens of vendors hawking some of the city's most excellent selection of Thai treats.

64 NANG LOENG

Nakhon Sawan Soi 6
Rattanakosin Island ③
+66 (0)81 513 1638

This is one of the oldest markets in Bangkok, worth coming to just to check out the outstanding single dish vendors who have been operating for generations. Foodie tours are slowly starting to come here, but the market sees relatively few tourists. In the middle there is a covered food court with just about every Thai dish under the sun available.

65 LANG SUAN MARKET

Langsuan Road
(betw Soi 2 and Soi 6)
Pathumwan ①

This food court, sandwiched in two small alleys leading off of Lang Suan, serves thousands of office workers from the surrounding embassy and business area, and features some of Bangkok's best *khao rat gaeng* rice and curry stalls. Avoid the 12-1 lunch rush, when you'll be hard pressed to find a seat.

62 OR TOR KOR

The 5 best places for
SUNDAY BRUNCH

66 **UP AND ABOVE**
AT: THE OKURA PRESTIGE HOTEL
57 Witthayu (Wireless) Road
Pathumwan ①
+66 (0)2 687 9000
www.okurabangkok.com

Alaskan king crab, Boston lobster, razor clams, fine imported cheeses, and enough sweets to feed an army, your only worry here will be your ability to walk out still standing. It's up on the 24th floor of the swank Okura Prestige, and the outdoor terrace views are almost as delectable as the food.

67 **BRASSERIE EUROPA**
AT: SIAM KEMPINSKI HOTEL
991/9 Rama I Road
Pathumwan ①
+66 (0)2 162 9000
www.kempinski.com/en/bangkok/siam-hote

Not only is it an all you can eat buffet of both Asian and European dishes, this is Bangkok's longest brunch fest, going on until 5 pm, meaning you can eat, go for a swim, and come back and eat again. It's also the only free flow champagne deal in town. Kids can also use the Siam Kempinski's Kid's Club for free as part of the deal.

68 VIU

AT: ST. REGIS HOTEL
159 Rajadamri Road
Pathumwan ①
+66 (0)2 207 7819
www.stregisbangkok.com/
fb_viu

From imported oysters to king crab and even foie gras, nothing is spared at perhaps Bangkok's most opulent Sunday brunch buffet. There is Peking duck, roast beef, and a cake section that you'll somehow have to find room for. There are not too many tables here, so best reserve if you want to join in the gluttony.

69 THEO MIO

AT: INTERCONTINENTAL HOTEL
973 Ploenchit Road
Pathumwan ①
+66 (0)2 656 0444
www.bangkok.
intercontinental.com/
best-italian-restaurant-
theo-mio

This Italian kitchen in the InterContinental Hotel serves up a tantalising Sunday Brunch. There are Italian antipasti favourites, along with endless tiramisu and free flow wine. However, you are limited to one main course item. There is a pleasant outdoor terrace and live jazz to complete the scene.

70 RAIN TREE CAFE

AT: PLAZA ATHÉNÉE HOTEL
61 Witthayu (Wireless)
Road
Pathumwan ①
+66 (0)2 650 8800
www.plazaathenee
bangkok.com/en/
restaurant/theraintreecafe

Set in the elegant Plaza Athénée. The Sunday brunch here offers a selection of Chinese, Japanese, Thai, and Western dishes to stuff yourself on. High end seared duck, grilled lamb, *fin de claire* oysters, and caviar are just a fraction of the quality favourites available here.

5 places for a delicious
HEALTHY MEAL

71 **DRESSED**
AT: MERCURY VILLE MALL
540 Ploenchit Road
Pathumwan ①
+66 (0)2 658 6688
www.dressedthailand.com

Named after the motto 'you are what you eat', Dressed serves 'create-your-own' salads, sandwiches, wraps and smoothies, all with the focus on healthy and fresh. It's clean, bright, and as it's already a well-known chain in the U.S., has plenty of fans here looking to escape sugar, MSG, and other no-no's.

72 **BREKKIE**
6/9 Soi Promsri,
Sukhumvit Soi 39
Sukhumvit ⑦
+66 (0)83 656 6141
www.brekkiebangkok.com

A glass balcony and cosy niches give Brekkie a designer feel, and the restaurant is aimed at iPhone wielding vegans. They substitute quinoa for fried rice, do grease free pancakes, sweet potato fries, and organic coffee, so you're sure to find something to feel healthy about here.

73 **FARM FACTORY**
AT: SILOM COMPLEX BUILDING
191 Silom Road
Silom/Bang Rak②
+66 (0)93 279 2796

Super healthy organic vegetable salads are what Farm Factory is all about. You can customise your own bowls here, adding quinoa, sun-dried tomatoes, pecans, and extra veggies. Organic cold pressed juices complement the salads.

74 ABSOLUTE FIT

AT: THE PORTICO
LIFESTYLE MALL
31 Langsuan Road
Pathumwan ①
+66 (0)81 371 3721
www.absolutefitfood.com

The team behind Absolute Yoga run this operation, which mainly serves as a healthy meal delivery service for those who are too busy to cook, but their cute little eatery in Lang Suan serves up über-healthy lunches like salmon risotto and green curry quinoa. Absolute Fit uses lots of spirulina, wakame, chia seeds, and goji berries in many of its dishes, making it pretty unique for Bangkok.

75 BROCCOLI REVOLUTION

899 Sukhumvit Road
Sukhumvit ⑦
+66 (0)2 662 5001

The owner runs the famed Monsoon restaurants in Yangon and Ho Chi Minh, but here takes a healthier focus, with an east-meets-west menu featuring quinoa burgers with guacamole, Vietnamese pho, and hummus mezze platters accompanied by hand pressed veggie juices. Hanging plants and huge windows looking out onto Sukhumvit are an added plus.

5

INDIAN

restaurants

---

76 **INDUS**
71 Sukhumvit Soi 26
Sukhumvit ⑦
+66 (0)2 258 4900
www.indusbangkok.com

Indus raises the bar for Indian fine dining, serving up traditional northern Indian cuisine with plenty of modern twists. Touted chef Anil Kumar whips up Laal Maas spicy mutton curry and succulent Tawa lobster, and the Raan leg of lamb marinated in spiced yogurt is a menu staple. The restaurant is set in a 1960s wooden art deco house.

77 **CHARCOAL TANDOOR GRILL & MIXOLOGY**
AT: FRASER SUITES
SUKHUMVIT, 5TH FLOOR
Sukhumvit Soi 11
Sukhumvit ⑦
+66 (0)89 307 1111
www.charcoalbkk.com

Indian market sounds piped into the restrooms are just part of the whimsical fun 'dining' that differentiates Charcoal from the other traditional Indian restaurants in town. Mutton kebabs braised in vinegar, cinnamon, and black cumin get washed down with Delhi Duty Free rum cocktails that are served in duty-free bags, just part of the playful takes here.

78 RANG MAHAL

AT: REMBRANDT HOTEL
19 Sukhumvit Soi 18
Sukhumvit ⑦
+66 (0)2 261 7100
www.rembrandtbkk.com/
restaurants

You are in maharaja territory here, truly elegant Indian fine dining. Crystal chandeliers, divans, Indian tapestries, and a fine 26th-floor city view enhance the regal and pricey meals. Don't miss the Kashimiri Rogan Josh, a succulent goat curry.

79 BAWARCHI

AT: PRESIDENT TOWER
973 Ploenchit Road
Pathumwan ①
+66 (0)2 656 0102
www.bawarchiindian.com

With two decades of experience, Bawarchi has a firm handle on excellent Indian cuisine. They specialise not only in traditional Mughlai cuisine, but also do a fusion tasting menu aimed at the Thai market, with unique items like tandoori *tom yum goong* or saffron and Thai basil risotto.

80 THE GREAT KABAB FACTORY

AT: THE MAJESTIC
GRANDE HOTEL
12 Sukhumvit Soi 2
Sukhumvit ⑦
+66 (0)2 262 2999
www.thegreatkabab
factory.com

This novel restaurant has branches across India, and brings new meaning and flavour to the world of kababs. There are over 450 of them on the menu, covering every spectrum of Indian cooking. You can choose from a set menu or à la carte, and the waiters explain each kabab and which chutney sauce is best to dip each one in.

5 great places for
BREAKFAST

---

81 CHU CHOCOLATE BAR & CAFE

AT: EXCHANGE TOWER, 2ND FLOOR

388 Sukhumvit Road
Sukhumvit ⑦
+66 (0)2 663 4554

All day brunch, homemade pancakes, French toast, and eggs Benedict are just a few reasons to hit up Bangkok's best breakfast nook. Chu is also renowned for its hot chocolate, perhaps the best in Asia, along with a great pastry selection.

82 CRÊPES & CO.

AT: 9:53 COMMUNITY MALL

124 Sukhumvit Soi 53
Thonglor/Ekkamai ⑧
+66 (0)2 726 9398
www.crepesnco.com

The 350-item menu features a staggering array of crepes, from traditional French to fusion Thai, from sweet to spicy. There's an all day brunch, plenty of items for non-crepe eaters, and even a kids' corner, making it perfect for families.

83 ROAST COFFEE AND EATERY

AT: THE COMMONS

335 Thonglor Soi 17
(Sukhumvit Soi 55)
Thonglor/Ekkamai ⑧
+66 (0)2 185 2865
www.roastbkk.com

Huevos rancheros and cranberry brioche French toast head a long list of high quality 'comfort food' breakfast items at this casual all-day eatery that is also known as being one of the best coffee roasters in town. The sleek setting in the trendy Thonglor Commons is an added plus.

84 ROCKET COFFEEBAR

147 Sathorn Soi 12
Sathorn ⑥
+66 (0)2 635 0404
www.rocketcoffeebar.com

Fancy takes on waffles (quail egg and truffle), herbed omelettes served with Gravlax salmon, and Swedish smørrebrød open sandwiches are all part of Rocket's stylish breakfast. The homey eatery has several branches, but the Sathorn location is the most charming. Make sure to sample the Rocket Fuel, a gourmet cold brew coffee.

85 TOOK LAE DEE

AT: FOODLAND
87 Sukhumvit Soi 5
Sukhumvit ⑦
+66 (0)2 254 2247
www.foodland.co.th

The name means 'cheap but good' in Thai, and that pretty much sums up this institution. The food isn't anything to rave about, but if you want a huge American breakfast with eggs, bacon, and toast at one of Bangkok's cheapest prices, this is ground zero. Food is served at a counter inside the Foodland Supermarket.

84 ROCKET COFFEEBAR

The 5 best restaurants
ON THE
CHAO PHRAYA RIVER

86 **STEVE CAFE**
68 Sri Ayutthaya Soi 21
Dusit ⑩
+66 (0)84 361 4910
www.stevecafeand
cuisine.com

Set in a half century-old house with a wooden deck right on the river, Steve's is hard to spot unless you come by river ferry, as well as being far enough up the Chao Phraya to be off the tourist track. Despite the name, it is Thai run, serving authentic southern Thai dishes to accompany the superb sunset and river views.

87 **SHEEPSHANK PUBLIC HOUSE**
47 Phra Athit Road
Banglamphu ⑨
+66 (0)2 629 5165
www.sheepshank
publichouse.com

Set in a former boat repair shop now decked out in industrial decor, you can feast on organic fusion creations like octopus and creamed corn risotto or rack of lamb with caramelised persimmons while gazing out at the Phra Athit pier and river traffic passing by.

88 **SALA RIM NAM**
AT: MANDARIN ORIENTAL
48 Oriental Avenue
Silom/Bang Rak ②
+66 (0)2 659 9000
www.mandarinoriental.
com/bangkok

Fine Thai dining complete with traditional costumed dancers in a beautiful old teak house make the Mandarin Oriental's signature Thai restaurant one of the most attractive spots along the river. You need to take the hotel shuttle boat over to the Thonburi side to get here.

89 SUPATRA RIVER HOUSE

266 Soi Wat Rakhang
Thonburi ⑤
+66 (0)2 411 0305
www.supatra
riverhouse.net

Set across the river from the Grand Palace in the former home of Mrs. Supatra, who founded the river ferry company and was a leading Thai businesswoman, this romantic spot has an outdoor terrace and air-conditioned indoor section overlooking the river. There is traditional Thai dance performed during dinner on Saturdays.

90 CHON

AT: THE SIAM HOTEL
3/2 Khao Road
Dusit ⑩
+66 (0)2 206 6999
www.thesiamhotel.com/
chon-thai-restaurant

The lovely old teak houses here once hosted Jackie Kennedy and Henry Ford, as they were owned by antique dealer and OSS agent Connie Mangksau. Today they are part of the Siam Hotel, Bangkok's most exclusive property, and home to the hotel's signature restaurant. Refined Thai dining goes hand in hand with the riverside location.

86 STEVE CAFE

The 5 best places for
S E A F O O D

---

91 CRAB AND CLAW
AT: THE EMQUARTIER, HELIX
QUARTIER, 7TH FLOOR
637 Sukhumvit Road
Sukhumvit ⑦
+66 (0)96 197 5769

Crab and Claw imports fresh, sustainable lobsters from Maine and serves the most authentic lobster roll, Old Bay-marinated crab, and clam chowder that you'll find in Southeast Asia. The restaurant is a massive hit for Thais, with crowds happily grinning with their stained lobster bibs on for endless Instagram-worthy snaps.

92 LEK & RUT SEAFOOD
49 Phadungdao Road,
Yaowarat
Chinatown ④
+66 (0)81 637 5039

This Chinatown legend is open-air, out on a corner in the heart of Yaowarat. It has become very touristy with prices to match, but the frenetic energy, with strangers all bunched together on plastic stools enjoying huge plates of prawns and crab, is well worth an evening out.

93 LEK SEAFOOD
Naradhiwas
Rajanagarindra Soi 3
Silom/Bang Rak ②
+66 (0)2 636 6460

If you are looking for tasty seafood in a no frills local eatery, then make a beeline for Lek. Despite being in the central business district, prices are kept even lower than Chinatown, and Thais flock here after work for the grilled and stir-fried fish, crab, and prawns.

SOMBOON SEAFOOD

169/7-12 Surawong Road
Silom/Bang Rak ②
+66 (0)2 223 3104
www.somboonseafood.com

94

Somboon is famed for its red curry crab and was one of the first seafood restaurants in town to become really popular. Some think the quality has gone down these days, but the original Surawong branch still serves up generous portions of fresh fish, prawns, and other seafood platters.

LAEM CHAROEN

AT: SIAM PARAGON, 4TH FLOOR
991 Rama I Road
Pathumwan ①
+66 (0)2 610 9244
www.laemcharoen
seafood.com

95

For almost 40 years, Thais have equated fresh seafood with Laem Charoen. The restaurant started out on the beach in Rayong, and now has some 15 outlets. This latest more upscale eatery in Siam Paragon retains its talents, with the fried sea bass being one of the best in town.

92 LEK & RUT SEAFOOD

5 wonderful
ITALIAN
restaurants

96 **IL BOLOGNESE**
139/3 Sathorn Soi 7
Sathorn ⑥
+66 (0)2 286 8805
www.ilbolognese
bangkok.com

Hidden down a small alleyway behind all of Sathorn's skyscrapers is this homey hideaway with superb hospitality and outstanding Italian cuisine. The pasta is homemade, and the amiable owner stops at every table to check on diners, bringing a free gelato as a palate cleanser between dishes, as well as a gratis tipple of limoncello to finish things off.

97 **APPIA**
20/4 Sukhumvit Soi 31
Sukhumvit ⑦
+66 (0)2 261 2056
www.appia-bangkok.com

Five-star chef Paolo Vitaletti and *Atlantic Monthly* food critic Jarred Wrisley are the partners behind Bangkok's only authentic Roman trattoria. Vitaletti, whose father was a butcher in Rome's meat market, serves up family recipes like organic porchetta rolled in fennel pollen and roasted on a rotisserie, and the wine list highlights small producers from around the Mediterranean.

98 PEPPINA

27/1 Sukhumvit Soi 33
Sukhumvit ⑦
+66 (0)2 119 7677
www.peppinabkk.com

Peppina takes pizza seriously. The flour, sea salt, and yeast dough here have risen for at least 24 hours, are opened by hand and then exquisitely crafted into some of the most epicurean pizza you will find in Asia. Besides the traditional pies, order a plate of the recommended mantaneras, which are stuffed with aged sheep's cheese.

99 JOJO

AT: ST. REGIS HOTEL
159 Rajadamri Road
Pathumwan ①
+66 (0)2 207 7815
*www.stregisbangkok.com/
fb_jojo*

Jojo excels at combining fine dining and authentic Italian. The candlelit patio and stylish dining room is one of Bangkok's most romantic spots to indulge in plates like D.O.P. Burrata cheese and rocket salad with a generous portion of melt-in-your-mouth cream or black truffle fettuccine. Additionally, the restaurant often plays host to guest Michelin-starred chefs.

100 ZANOTTI II

AT: SALADAENG COLONNADE
21/2 Saladaeng Road
Silom/Bang Rak ②
+66 (0)2 636 0002
*www.zanotti-
ristorante.com*

Zanotti is in its second decade, which is about two decades longer than most Italian restaurants here. They still do old-fashioned classics without the twists, concentrating on homemade pasta, good wines, and a stylish environment which caters to the business district location crowd.

The 5 best
MEXICAN
restaurants

---

101 LA MONITA URBAN CANTINA
AT: THE EMQUARTIER, HELIX QUARTIER, 7TH FLOOR
637 Sukhumvit Road
Sukhumvit ⑦
+66 (0)2 003 6238
www.lamonita.com/
emquartier/#mexican-
urban-cantina

La Monita elevates Mexican cuisine to new heights. You won't find tacos and burritos here; instead, feast on *alambra mar y tierra* made with New Zealand ribeye, ceviche served with wasabi and Peruvian *leche de tigre*, and homemade sausage *longanizoqueso*. They also have a mixologist whipping up homemade sangrias and a trendy spot overlooking the gourmet food floor of Bangkok's glitziest mall.

102 MEJICO
AT: GROOVE@ CENTRALWORLD, LEVEL 2
999/9 Rama I Road
Pathumwan ①
+66 (0)2 252 6660

Mejico is a branch of an Australian chain that focuses on being a hip tequila bar offering an array of Mexican and Latin tapas-style bites. There's a raw bar with ceviche and fusion pulled pork tacos, and the Mexican-influenced cocktails are staggering.

103 BARRIO BONITO
AT: THE COMMONS
355 Thonglor Soi 17
Thonglor/Ekkamai ⑧
+66 (0)2 712 7832
www.barriobonito.com

This grandma's cooking simple Mexican spot was a legend when it ran for seven years on Koh Chang island. The owners have since relocated to the gourmet Commons food court in Thonglor, bringing their excellent food to Bangkok.

104 THE SLANTED TACO

Sukhumvit Soi 23
Sukhumvit ⑦
+66 (0)2 258 0546
www.slantedtaco.com

The owner prides his kitchen on making everything from scratch and aims to create authentic Mexican combined with a Miami South Beach vibe. It's a cheery spot where you can sample hard to find pozole corn soup or go straight to the classic burritos and tacos, and the location next to a craft beer bar couldn't be more appetising.

105 THE MISSING BURRO

145 Soi Sing Waet Lom,
Thonglor Soi 7
Thonglor/Ekkamai ⑧
+66 (0)90 913 2131
www.themissingburro.com

Bangkok Mexican tends to mostly be Tex Mex, and combining this with the trendy Thonglor restaurant scene can easily fail to live up to the hype, but the two Mexican brothers running the cantina serve up truly authentic Yucatan-influenced cuisine, set in a funky pair of converted shipping containers with garden seating out front as well.

101 LA MONITA URBAN CANTINA

5 tropical
THAI FRUITS
you must try

---

106 RAMBUTAN

This exotic fruit is named after the Malay word for 'hairy', and indeed it features a hairy red peel with soft spikes. When opened, it reveals a soft white fruit that looks much like a lychee. Thailand is the largest producer of rambutan in the world, with almost 600.000 tonnes of them grown per year.

107 SALAK

Known as snake fruit, due to its reptilian skin, salak comes from a palm tree, and the fruit has a powerful sour and sweet interior, tasting quite acidic on first bite, followed by a honey-like sweetness. In Bangkok, vendors will often give you a small bag of sugar to dip your pods into.

108 JACKFRUIT

Don't confuse the spiky exterior of this giant fruit with the durian. Although they look the same on the outside, the inside is completely different, with the jackfruit being filled with small yellow pods that have no strong odour, and are incredibly sweet and sticky.

109 DURIAN

Called the 'king of fruit' by many, you'll either love it or hate it. Durians have a ridiculously pungent aroma, such that you will see signs in hotels and on trains in Thailand that ban them from being brought inside. However, the inside of the spiky durian contains a custard-like soft creamy flesh that really is superb when ripe. For those who find the consistency off-putting, try it in a milkshake, where it really excels.

110 MANGOSTEEN

A popular tourist favourite. Mangosteens have a hard purple outside, with orange-like white sections inside, which are extremely sweet and full of vitamin C. The prime season for them is the winter cool period, from December through February, but these days you can usually find some year-round. Make sure not to eat the large seeds, as they are very bitter.

109 DURIAN

MOON BAR

75 PLACES
FOR A DRINK

The 5 coolest
BARS FOR COCKTAILS

---

111 VESPER
10/15 Convent Road
Silom/Bang Rak ②
+66 (0)2 235 2777
www.vesperbar.co

Named #1 bar in Thailand and #17 in all Asia in 2016, Vesper is named after James Bond's favourite martini and specialises in amazing cocktails, from barrel-aged Negronis to sharing cocktails to creative drinks like Ketel One vodka mixed with homemade yoghurt and blueberries.

112 IL FUMO
1098/2 Rama IV Road
Sathorn ⑥
+66 (0)2 286 8833
www.ilfumo.com

Housed in a former king's villa, you recline on leather armchairs while choosing between bespoke tableside martini service or the house's stiff old-fashioned drinks that consistently win awards on the Bangkok drinking scene. Il Fumo is a fine Italian restaurant as well, should you get hungry while drinking.

113 VOGUE LOUNGE
AT: MAHANAKHON CUBE,
6TH FLOOR
96 Naradhiwas
Rajanagarindra Road
Sathorn ⑥
+66 (0)2 001 0697
www.voguelounge.com

This just might be the best bar in Bangkok, combining creative drinks from ace bartender Francesco Moretti along with a setting right out of a black and white 1960's *Vogue Magazine* shoot, as well as the city's only air-conditioned outdoor deck.

114 RARB

49 Phra Athit Road
Banglamphu ⑨
+66 (0)81 406 3773

Karn Liangsrisuk, a former Thai Best Bartending Awards winner, is the star behind the counter at this hole-in-the-wall riverside bar. Karn is a virtual walking encyclopaedia of mixology, turning homecrafted infusions, fresh fruit from markets, and alcohol into sublime drinks. The simple paper menu features outrageously named concoctions like My Lovely Whore and F**k My Farm.

115 HAVANA SOCIAL

Sukhumvit Soi 11
Sukhumvit ⑦
+66 (0)61 450 3750

The interior resembles pre-revolution Havana, complete with cracked ceilings and retro furniture (straight out of Fidel's younger days), and there are great mojitos and rum drinks on the menu, plus Cuban dancing on weekends. You need to call the bar in advance and get an entry code, which you punch into the old retro payphone booth outside.

113 VOGUE LOUNGE

The 5 liveliest
DANCE CLUBS

---

116 **LEVELS**
AT: ALOFT HOTEL, 6TH FLOOR
35 Sukhumvit Soi 11
Sukhumvit ⑦
+66 (0)82 308 3246
www.levelsclub.com

Levels leads the charge on party street Sukhumvit Soi 11. This is the top club on the street and in the area, with huge international DJ acts taking charge over a massive sound system and LED lighting show. There is a huge dance area plus a terrace bar to hang out in.

117 **CÉ LA VI**
AT: SATHORN SQUARE TOWER,
39TH FLOOR
98 Sathorn Square,
North Sathorn Road
Sathorn ⑥
+66 (0)2 108 2000
www.celavi.com

You are going to pay to drink and party here, but you get a magnificent city view from the 39th floor location, and this is where the moneyed and pretty come to let loose. If you get a sense of *déjà vu*, it's because the club used to be the swank Ku De Ta, now with a different name, part of a chain across Asia.

118 **ROUTE 66**
Royal City Avenue,
29/33-48 Soi Soonvijai,
Rama IX Road
Northern Bangkok ⑦
+66 (0)2 203 0936
www.route66club.com

Route 66 is a legendary Bangkok dance club. It sits along the RCA Strip, which is where young Thais come to party. As a foreigner, you'll pay 300 baht to enter here, and the crowd is 90% Thai. Route 66 has a fun vibe, with one room featuring live bands and another playing techno and hip-hop.

119 ONYX

**Royal City Avenue, Soi
Soonvijai, Rama IX Road
Northern Bangkok ⑦
+66 (0)81 645 1166**
www.onyxbangkok.com

Featuring one of Bangkok's biggest dance floors (2500-person capacity), plus private VIP booths if you want to dance to your own party, Onyx specialises in laser shows, confetti bombs, and international DJs spinning house music. It is the most sophisticated club along the youngster party zone street of RCA.

120 DEMO

**Thonglor Soi 10
Thonglor/Ekkamai ⑧
+66 (0)85 250 2000**

This is the best place to check out moneyed-up young Thais out for an all-night party. Demo heads the list of pulsating clubs in trendy Thonglor. The multiple dance floors are located inside a graffiti-covered old warehouse, and hip-hop and techno keep the beautiful young crowd energised.

The 5 best
CAFES

---

121 **GALLERY DRIP COFFEE**
AT: BANGKOK ART & CULTURE
CENTRE
939 Rama I Road
Pathumwan ①
+66 (0)81 989 5244

The owners are a pair of photographers and coffee connoisseurs, and spend most of the day hunched over ceramic drip filters, fastidiously pouring slow jugs of single origin Ethiopian, Kenyan, and Thai organic beans. The artsy cafe draws in design lovers heading into the BAAC to view the latest exhibitions.

122 **ROOTS**
AT: THE COMMONS
Thonglor Soi 17,
Sukhumvit 55
Thonglor/Ekkamai ⑧
+66 (0)97 059 4517
www.rootsbkk.com

One of the original players involved in getting gourmet coffee going in Bangkok, Roots sources single origin beans from around the world as well as working with Thai farmers, and in addition to running this cafe, they do barista training and artisan coffee making workshops.

123 **INK & LION**
1/7 Ekkamai Soi 2,
Sukhumvit Soi 63
Thonglor/Ekkamai ⑧
+66 (0)91 559 0994

White brick walls and a comfy vibe make this place popular with digital nomads, who work on their computers over cups of espresso machine shots or hand-done pourovers. In addition to the artistic lattes, there are great pastries. Closed on Thursday and Friday.

124 CERESIA

593/29-41 Sukhumvit
Soi 33/1
Sukhumvit ⑦
+66 (0)98 251 4327
*www.ceresia
coffeeroasters.com*

We must thank two Venezuelan sisters (and one's Thai husband) for putting Bangkok firmly on the global coffee map. Lucia Aguilar and her sister come from a family of coffee growers in Latin America, and they know their stuff. The trio source the beans from single origin cooperatives around the world, and the owners love talking coffee with the clientele.

125 EIAH SAE

101-103 Padsai Road
Chinatown ④
+66 (0)2 221 0549

For nearly ninety years, this funky cafe with purple walls has been churning out the owner's great-grandparents' Thai-coffee recipes to a legion of faithful chain-smoking regulars, who look like they have been coming in since the cafe first opened. The cups of traditional *cafe boran* (ancient coffee) with sweet condensed milk are strong, and it's worth coming for the ambience alone.

125 EIAH SAE

The 5 best bars for
LIVE MUSIC

---

126 **ADHERE THE 13TH BLUES BAR**
13 Samsen Road
Banglamphu ⑨
+66 (0)89 769 4613

New bars come and go with the rains in Bangkok, but Adhere has been around for ages. Small, crowded, and very local, this musician-owned club specialises in live blues and jazz, with open mike nights alternating with organised shows. Drinks are cheap, and the atmosphere is old-school and fun-loving.

127 **SAXOPHONE PUB**
3/8 Phayathai Road,
Victory Monument
Northern Bangkok ⑪
+66 (0)2 246 5472
www.saxophonepub.com

One of Bangkok's most popular and long-running venues, Saxophone just celebrated its 30th anniversary. Noted Thai sax player Koh Mr. Saxman performs here regularly, as does the jamming T-Bone band, which plays reggae and brings down the house. It's an unpretentious and fun hangout, frequented equally by Thais and foreigners.

128 **BROWN SUGAR**
469 Phrasumen Road,
Bawornniwas
Rattanakosin Island ③
+66 (0)89 499 1378
www.brownsugar bangkok.com

Newsweek magazine wrote up Brown Sugar as 'one of the best bars in the world', and while the jazz club has relocated to more spacious digs since then, it still is noted for excellent live jazz performances and a mellow vibe.

129 **APOTEKA**
33/28 Sukhumvit Soi 11
Sukhumvit ⑦
+66 (0)61 881 8401

While the bar is supposed to resemble a 19th-century apothecary, with cocktails given names like 'Vaccination', nobody pays much attention to that here, as they are all bopping along to the stellar beats of the Keith Nolan or Soi Dog Blues Band, both of which perform regularly and churn out some of Bangkok's best blues.

130 **THE ROCK PUB**
AT: HOLLYWOOD STREET
BUILDING
93/26-28 Phayathai Road
Northern Bangkok ①
+66 (0)99 191 5666
www.therockpub-
bangkok.com

Bangkok youngsters tend to favour hip-hop and electronica, but The Rock Pub has been open for decades and remains Bangkok's only venue for those who like metal, grunge, and loud rock 'n' roll. There are rotating house bands along with the occasional foreign act, and the venue is dingy, hot, and wonderfully unpretentious.

126 ADHERE THE 13TH BLUES BAR

5 top
ROOFTOP BARS

131 **MOON BAR**
AT: BANYAN TREE HOTEL,
61ST FLOOR
**21/100 South Sathorn
Road
Sathorn ⑥
+66 (0)2 679 1200**
www.banyantree.com

The panoramas here are unrivalled, 360°
of nothing but endless skyscrapers and the
Bangkok lights. Completely exposed to the
elements, don't even think about coming
up here in bad weather. Photographers will
love it too, as it's the only sky bar that is
tripod friendly and lets you set up for those
great sunsets.

132 **SKY BAR**
AT: LEBUA STATE TOWER,
63RD FLOOR
**1055 Silom Road
Silom/Bang Rak ②
+66 (0)2 624 9555**
www.lebua.com/sky-bar

Located up on top of the Lebua Hotel and
State Tower, movie fans will recognise this
bar as being the scene shot in the Hollywood
comedy *Hangover II*. Yes, you can slurp down
a Hangovertini here, but the main reason to
come is the jaw-dropping view of the sunset
over the Chao Phraya River.

133 **OCTAVE**
AT: MARRIOTT HOTEL
**2 Sukhumvit Soi 57
Thonglor/Ekkamai ⑧
+66 (0)2 797 0000**
www.marriott.com

Most of Bangkok's rooftop bars are
surrounded by skyscrapers, but Octave
differentiates itself by being on top of one
of the few high rises on the east side of
town. The wooden deck up on the 45th
floor here boasts a 360° panorama, as well
as a unique look straight down the entire
sky train line below.

134 CRU AT RED SKY

AT: CENTARA GRAND,
58TH FLOOR
999/99 Rama I Road
Pathumwan ①
+66 (0)2 100 6255
www.champagnecru.com

The Red Sky Bar on the 55th floor of the Centara is nice enough, but head 3 more flights up to CRU, a champagne bar that is the highest rooftop bar in town. The views are dizzying here, and you can indulge in GH Mumm pink champagne. Every seat affords a 360° view of every landmark in Bangkok.

135 THE SPEAKEASY ROOFTOP BAR

AT: HOTEL MUSE, 24TH AND
25TH FLOOR
555 Langsuan Road
Pathumwan ①
+66 (0)2 630 4000
www.hotelmuse
bangkok.com

This elegant sky bar has two floors, one with more intimate tables for two along a small deck, and a more spacious rooftop area, with comfy chairs and sofas to relax in under the stars.

134 CRU AT RED SKY

The 5 most
ATMOSPHERIC
bars

---

136 SING SING THEATRE
Sukhumvit Soi 45
Sukhumvit ⑦
+66 (0)63 225 1331
www.singsingbangkok.com

Secret passages, lanterns on the ceiling, metal dragons, and dancing girls help give Sing Sing the look of an upscale Chinese bordello in the Roaring Twenties. There are pulsing live dance and DJ shows with multicoloured laser lighting, and the venue attracts a beautiful high society crowd.

137 SMALLS
186/3 Suan Phlu Soi 1
Sathorn ⑥
+66 (0)95 585 1398

David Jacobson, owner of the legendary Q Bar, has moved across town and opened this intimate and eclectic jazz and cocktail bar, which feels more like something one would find in Manhattan or Berlin. There is a traditional absinthe fountain, revolving doors, red velvet curtains, a dumbwaiter, a rooftop hangout, and a great vibe.

138 MAGGIE CHOO'S

320 Silom Road
Silom/Bang Rak ②
+66 (0)91 772 2144
www.maggiechoos.com

Yet another phantasmagorical creation by nightlife design deity Ashley Sutton. To enter, you go through a set of carved doors that disappear into a Cantonese noodle restaurant, then sneak behind a curtain into what used to be the vault room for the East India Company Bank, now full of swank black couches with golden cushions, surrounded by brick walls and steel vault doors.

139 THE IRON FAIRIES

402 Thonglor
(Sukhumvit Soi 55)
Thonglor/Ekkamai ⑧
+66 (0)99 918 1600

This is nightlife design mogul Ashley Sutton's first venue, inspired by his own fairytale book and little iron carved fairies that are for sale throughout the bar. The place is part blacksmith, part Alice in Wonderland maze, part factory, and yes, a smashingly good cocktail bar complete with iron staircases, and pixie dust flying about.

140 THE BAMBOO BAR

AT: MANDARIN ORIENTAL
48 Oriental Avenue
Silom/Bang Rak ②
+66 (0)2 659 9000
www.mandarin
oriental.com

For over half a century the Bamboo Bar has been an institution. Home to jazz artists (Ray Charles and Louis Armstrong played here), fine drinks, and a moody interior that looks like a cross between a colonial whisky hideout and African safari retreat.

5 bars to visit
ON THE RIVERSIDE

141 AMOROSA BAR
AT: ARUN RESIDENCE
**36-38 Soi Pratu
Nokyung
Rattanakosin Island ③
+66 (0)2 221 9158**
www.arunresidence.com

Few visitors know about this bar, accessed down a dead end lane next to the river, with views across to Wat Arun. The bar is upstairs from the Deck restaurant and Arun Residence, a tiny boutique hotel, and is a great place for a sunset drink, followed by the temple lights coming on as the light fades.

142 RIVER VIBE BAR
**768 Soi Phanurangsi,
Songwat Road
Chinatown ②
+66 (0)2 234 5429**
www.riverviewbkk.com

You'll have to look at their website to figure out how to get here; certainly no taxi driver will know it. This rooftop bar is completely hidden in a Chinatown riverside alleyway. You get the same river view as most of the nearby 5-star hotels at an absolute fraction of the price.

143 VIVA AVIV
AT: RIVER CITY
**23 Trok Rongnam-
khaeng, Yota Road
Chinatown ②
+66 (0)2 639 6305**
www.vivaaviv.com

One of the hippest modern bars set on the river. Fancy signature cocktails, superb views right over the water, and set at the back of River City, an antique mall where most of the river cruises leave from, so plenty of people-watching and activity going on out on the pier out front.

144 **THE ROOF**
AT: SALA RATTANAKOSIN
39 Maharat Road,
Soi Tha Tien
Rattanakosin Island ③
+66 (0)2 622 1388
www.salarattanakosin.com

Similar to the Amorosa, The Roof also looks out on Wat Arun, but is higher up, with a far superior view, and is most certainly more elegant. You can enjoy the sunset with signature cocktails like the Chao Phraya gin fizz or The River, made with Absolut vodka and Blue Curacao.

145 **ANANTARA LONGTAIL BAR**
AT: ANANTARA RIVERSIDE
BANGKOK
257/1-3 Charoennakorn
Road
Thonburi ⑤
+66 (0)2 476 0022
www.bangkok-riverside.
anantara.com/longtail-bar

Set away from the crowds south of the city, the Longtail gives uninterrupted river views with the Bangkok skyline in the back. Kick back to a Bangkok Bridge (gin and lychee cocktail) and watch the teak shuttle boats make their way across the river.

144 THE ROOF

The 5 smoothest
SPEAKEASIES

---

146 J. BOROSKI
**Sukhumvit Soi 55
(Thonglor, before Soi 7)
Thonglor/Ekkamai ⑧
+66 (0)2 712 6025**

Joseph Boroski bills himself as a 'mixsultant', and the Manhattan cocktail guru is known around the world. This is his own private speakeasy, hidden in a dead end alley. Contact him via Facebook or make an effort with Google maps to find the bar. There isn't a menu, you just tell the bartenders what alcohol you like and they will create a drink for you.

147 Q & A BAR
**235/13 Sukhumvit Soi
21 (Asoke)
Sukhumvit ⑦
+66 (0)2 664 1445
*www.qnabar.com***

Q & A is a tiny bar that has no sign outside, just a question mark on the entrance door. Inside, the bar consists of a row of leather seats that lines a bar resembling a 1920s American railway car. A trio of superb bartenders serve up non-orthodox takes on classic drinks.

148 RABBIT HOLE
**125 Sukhumvit Soi 55
(Thonglor)
Thonglor/Ekkamai ⑧
+66 (0)98 969 1335**

Lots of bartenders drink here on their day off, and the drinks really stand out. The Casa Nostra is like an Old Fashioned, only it has a smoked cigar taste added to it. Like other speakeasies in town, there is no sign outside, just look for the sliding door next to the Ainu Japanese bar.

149 BACKSTAGE COCKTAIL BAR
AT: PLAYHAUS THONGLOR
205/22-23 Sukhumvit
Soi 55
Thonglor/Ekkamai ⑧
+66 (0)61 519 5891

Kitibordee 'Gov' Chortubtim, one of the finalists at the Diageo Southeast Asia Bartending World Championships, heads the stellar team of mixologists here, designing drinks like the Earthbeet, which combines beetroot infused tequila with sweet vermouth, Campari and artichoke liqueur, along with torched liquorice. The bar itself resembles a backstage dressing room in a burlesque theatre.

150 THE LOCKER ROOM
AT: JIA FOOD MALL
Thonglor Soi 10
Thonglor/Ekkamai ⑧
+66 (0)92 895 3689

This amazing speakeasy hides behind a row of lockers parked out in the back of Chinese restaurant Ping's. You slide open a wall panel and dark curtains and leather sofas welcome you to the abode of four of Asia's leading bartenders, who concoct exquisite drinks like the Bloodless Maria, a clear mezcal take on the Bloody Mary.

146 J. BOROSKI

The 5 best
CRAFT BEER
bars

---

151 HAIR OF THE DOG

**593/27 Sukhumvit
(betw Soi 33/1 and Soi
Villa Market)
Sukhumvit ⑦
+66 (0)2 258 1461**
www.hairofthedogbkk.com

There are 13 rotating taps here of some of the best craft beers in the world, along with hundreds of great bottles as well. The venue resembles a speakeasy, with beer geeks on every stool. The suds don't come cheap, but ladies can get 50% off on taps on Tuesday nights.

152 MIKKELLER

**26 Ekkamai Soi 10,
Yeak 2
Thonglor/Ekkamai ⑧
+66 (0)2 381 9891**
*www.mikkeller
bangkok.com*

You'll need to use their website instructions to find this place, it is that hidden, which is all part of Mikkeller's plan. They don't want walk-in traffic, only real craft beer lovers. With 30 rotating taps and countless specialised bottle selections, they are one of the best options in Bangkok.

153 BOTTLES OF BEER

**2/7 Sukhumvit Soi 34
Sukhumvit ⑦
+66 (0)2 040 0473**
www.bottlesofbeer.co

Besides featuring the owner's adorable chihuahua having the run of the place, this tiny bar has a huge global selection of craft beers, along with a wholesale discounts applied when you order 6 or more bottles, making it one of the cheapest craft spots in town.

154 **WISHBEER HOME BAR**
1491 Sukhumvit
(at Soi 67)
Sukhumvit ⑦
+66 (0)2 392 1403
www.wishbeerhomebar.com

Located in a cavernous former elevator factory warehouse, Wishbeer has gone from an online beer delivery service to a relaxing hangout, with 18 taps of beer and the best happy hour craft beer prices in town. They have a staggering collection of over 200 bottles from around the world, and you can buy bottles to take home.

155 **GOLDEN COINS TAPROOM**
AT: EKKAMAI MALL
3 Ekkamai Soi 10
Thonglor/Ekkamai ⑧
+66 (0)82 675 9673

This is one of Bangkok's first Thai craft beer bars. Due to draconian laws, they can't brew their own on the premises, but they get around this by brewing in Vietnam and then shipping the beer back. It's nice to have a local spot in an industry that tends to be foreign dominated.

5 great places to have a
DRINK IN CHINATOWN

---

156 **TEENS OF THAILAND**
    76 Soi Nana
    Chinatown ④
    +66 (0)96 846 0506

Hidden behind a couple of thick wooden doors, this is a gin lovers paradise. Ace mixologist bartender Niks Anuman-Rajadhon is renowned for his infused gins and creative takes on the G & T such as chrysanthemum or Thai iced tea gin and tonics.

157 **TEP BAR**
    69-71 Soi Rammaitri,
    Maitrijit Road
    Chinatown ④
    +66 (0)98 467 2944

Tep Bar is set inside of a traditional two-storey Chinese shophouse, with mood lighting and tatami cushioned floor tables to relax on upstairs. The bar specialises in traditional Thai white spirits, known as ya dong, making their own upscale version, and serving up either platters of different shots or creatively mixed cocktails.

158 **SOULBAR**
    945 Charoenkrung Road
    Chinatown ②
    +66 (0)93 220 0441

SoulBar bucks the trend of quiet hidden niches in Chinatown. The bar is tiny, there's barely room to dance, and yet dance everyone does, with thumping soul and funk sets each night entertaining the crowd, which spills out the door of the shophouse on weekends.

159 EL CHIRINGUITO
221 Soi Nana
Chinatown ④
+66 (0)85 126 0046

This hole-in-the-wall bar's original function was as a tapas bar, and the Thai owner's several year stint in Spain makes it resemble something right out of Barcelona. You can nibble on bocadillos, but the real treat are the array of Xoriguer gin drinks that they serve.

160 23 BAR & GALLERY
92 Soi Nana
Chinatown ④
+66 (0)80 264 4471

The owner here ran a cult-status bar in the Sukhumvit area for years, named Bar 23. Rents got far too pricey there, so he's joined the artsy community on the fringes of Chinatown and set up a no frills joint that has cheap drinks and plays rock 'n' roll tunes.

156 **TEENS OF THAILAND**

5 *drinks*
YOU MUST TRY
IN BANGKOK

---

161 **SIAM MARY**
AT: ST. REGIS HOTEL/BAR
159 Ratchadamri Road
Pathumwan ①
+66 (0)2 207 7826
www.stregisbangkok.com/
en/fb_bar

The Bloody Mary was first created at the St. Regis in New York in 1934, and Bangkok's Regis Bar has done their own interpretation of it, throwing in Thai chilies, coriander, lemongrass, and Thai basil, giving it enough spice to match the hot surroundings it is served in.

162 **F**K MY FARM**
AT: RARB
49 Phra Athit Road
Banglamphu ⑨
+66 (0)81 406 3773

An array of fresh fruit infused alcohol dominates this outstanding drink, whipped up by Bangkok's most creative bartender, Karn Liangrisuk, award winner and one of the founders at Rarb Bar. You'll have to watch him make it to even hope to understand what is in it.

163 **HANGOVERTINI**
AT: SKY BAR, LEBUA STATE
TOWER, 63RD FLOOR
1055 Silom Road
Silom/Bang Rak ②
+66 (0)2 624 9555
www.lebua.com/sky-bar

Served at the Sky Bar at the Lebua and named after the Hollywood film shot here, the Hangovertini combines Chivas, sweet vermouth, honey infused rosemary, and a drop of matcha green tea syrup along with apple juice to win over movie buffs and drinkers alike.

164 **LYCHEEGRASS COLLINS**
AT: SOUL FOOD MAHANAKORN
56/10 Sukhumvit Soi 55
Thonglor ⑧
+66 (0)2 714 7708
www.soulfood
mahanakorn.com

This Tom Collins spin off combines Beefeater Gin with lychee liqueur, fresh lemongrass, and lime, turning it into a soothing tropical refreshment. It's part of the Thai based cocktails meant to pair up with food at the popular Soul Food Mahanakorn.

165 **THE TOM KHA GAI**
AT: REVOLUCION COCKTAIL
50 Suksawittaya,
Sathorn Soi 10
Silom/Bang Rak ②
+66 (0)2 235 4823

Revolucion Cocktail makes this one, mixing lemongrass, kaffir lime, coconut puree, lime juice, and *galanga* (Thai ginger) syrup. That's everything in the favourite Thai dish except the chicken! The bartender's cocktail tossing tricks make it even more enjoyable as well.

161 SIAM MARY

The 5 best
ALTERNATIVE
NIGHTLIFE venues

---

166 SOI COWBOY
betw Sukhumvit Soi
21 and 23 Sukhumvit
Sukhumvit ⑦

This narrow alley full of hostess bars allegedly was named after its first foreign bar owner, who wore a cowboy hat. Of all the Bangkok red light areas, it's the preferred hangout for expats, as drink prices are clearly marked and there is little hassle or scamming to deal with.

167 PATPONG
Patpong Soi 2,
Silom Road
Silom/Bang Rak ②

Tourists combine visits to the adjacent night market with the obligatory gogo bar visit here. While the downstairs bars present little problem, keep away from the 'ping pong' show offers and any places where you go upstairs, as outrageous padded bills are the norm.

168 DJ STATION
8/6-8 Silom Soi 2
Silom/Bang Rak ②
+66 (0)2 266 4029
www.dj-station.com

One of Bangkok's longest running gay clubs, DJ Station is massive (three floors), pulsating, and sweaty. There is a cabaret drag show around 11 each night, and then it's shirts off wild dancing until the wee hours. It's a poser-dominated in-your-face crowd here, and most definitely isn't for the shy and squeamish.

169 TELEPHONE BAR

114/11-13 Silom Soi 4
Silom/Bang Rak ②
+66 (0)2 234 3279
www.telephonepub.com

Telephone has been here for over 25 years, and is the best known of all the gay venues on lively Soi 4. The bar is named Telephone Bar because it used to have phones at each table where you could call someone whom you liked across the room. The phones are gone, but there is still live music, karaoke, and a welcoming vibe.

170 WONG'S PLACE

27/3 Soi Sri Bamphen,
Rama IV Road
Sathorn ⑥
+66 (0)2 286 1558

Wong's is a legendary dive bar that tends to open after everything else in town is shut. It's not necessarily sleazy, pickup-oriented, gay, or any other label, but it attracts an eclectic mix of those who've probably been out drinking far too long already.

166 SOI COWBOY

The 5 most interesting
HAPPY HOURS

—————

171 **TUBA**
34 Ekkamai Soi 21 (Soi
Chamchan)
Thonglor/Ekkamai ⑧
+66 (0)2 711 5500

This retro bar, full of antiques and bric-à-brac that is all for sale, does a happy hour from 5 to 8 where all drinks are 2 for 1, and where the glasses they put them in are big enough for you to have a hard time lifting them up.

172 **REVOLUCION COCKTAIL**
50 Suksawittaya,
Sathorn Soi 10
Sathorn ⑥
+66 (0)2 235 4823
www.revolucion-cocktail.com

This is the first Bangkok branch of Revolucion, founded by Sebastien Bonnefoi, the mixology master who runs China's Urban Bar bartending school. They have a 50% off happy hour here before 8. Molecular and fire cocktails add plenty of excitement, and the Absolut vodka bottle-shaped swimming pool adds to the fun.

173 **WOO BAR**
AT: W HOTEL
106 North Sathorn Road
Sathorn ⑥
+66 (0)2 344 4000
www.whotelbangkok.com/woo_bar

The W Hotel's snazzy Woo Bar has purple neon design lighting and super comfy leather armchairs to sprawl on, but you aren't coming here just for the decor. Wednesday nights sees free flow sparkling wine for gents, Thursday sees 2 for 1 or freebie ladies nights, and there are plenty of other deals to be had.

174 JUNKER AND BAR
454 Suan Phlu Soi 1
Sathorn ⑥
+66 (0)85 100 3608

There's a half price discount on the well crafted cocktails from 5 to 6.30 pm as well as ladies night discounts on Saturdays at this funky bar, which sees the crowd spilling into the street each night. Part of the reason is the owner's homemade alcohol infusions, with great drinks at a fraction of the price you'll pay elsewhere in town.

175 AXIS & SPIN
AT: THE CONTINENT HOTEL,
38TH FLOOR
413 Sukhumvit Road
Sukhumvit ⑦
+66 (0)2 686 7000
www.thecontinentdining.
com/axis-and-spin.php

Not only do you get a stunning view of the Bangkok skyline from this 38th floor bar, but you also get a 2-for-1 drink special from 5 to 8 pm. The menu features an array of aptly named 'pre-prohibition, prohibition, and post-war' cocktails, and it is a suave spot to watch the sun go down.

1/2 REVOLUCION COCKTAIL

5 wonderful
TEAHOUSES

---

176 **DOUBLE DOGS TEA ROOM**
406 Yaowarat Road
Chinatown ④
+66 (0)86 329 3075

Chinatown's Yaowarat Road is always hectic, so this oasis of air-con and peace is a welcome relief. There are specialty loose leaf teas from around the world here, ranging from Japanese green matcha to blue Da Hong Pao and Oolong from China.

177 **THE COURTYARD**
AT: THE HOUSE ON SATHORN,
W HOTEL
106 North Sathorn Road
Sathorn ⑥
+66 (0)2 344 4025
*www.thehouseon
sathorn.com*

Set in the garden of the lovely 130-year-old colonial mansion House on Sathorn, The Courtyard has tables set around the exquisite architecture, which you can admire while you partake of the afternoon tea set, which is served daily from 2.30 to 5.30 pm and features scones with Devonshire clotted cream.

178 **1823**
AT: GAYSORN VILLAGE
999 Ploenchit Road
Pathumwan ①
+66 (0)2 656 1086
*www.1823ronnefeldt
bkk.com*

The seventh-generation Ronnefeldt tealounge from Germany has come to Bangkok, with this traditional European tealounge serving up some of the world's finest teas, along with German pastries, brunches, and a few Thai twists. Located in the elegant Gaysorn Shopping Mall, this is about as regal as afternoon tea gets in Bangkok.

179 ERAWAN TEA ROOM
AT: GRAND HYATT ERAWAN
494 Rajadamri Road
Pathumwan ①
+66 (0)2 254 6250
www.bangkok.grand.
hyatt.com/en/hotel/dining/
ErawanTeaRoom.html

Thai silks, porcelain vases, and old-school decor are part of noted designer Tony Chi's layout in the Grand Hyatt Erawan's lovely tearoom. They do an afternoon tea set with lovely pastries, and there is also an excellent Thai food menu if you get hungry. The tearoom overlooks the Erawan Shrine and busy Rajaprasong Junction.

180 AUTHOR'S LOUNGE
AT: MANDARIN ORIENTAL
48 Oriental Avenue
Silom/Bang Rak ②
+66 (0)2 659 9000
www.mandarinoriental.
com/bangkok/fine-dining/
authors-lounge/

Graham Greene and Somerset Maugham were guests in this 1870s building set in the Mandarin Oriental. While the hotel is expensive, a traditional afternoon tea set here won't wipe out your wallet, and you can marvel at the old black and white photos on the wall, and the couples coming in to do wedding shots at one of Bangkok's most photographed locations.

178 **1823**

The 5 best bars for
A GLASS OF WINE

—————

181 **WINE CONNECTION DELI & BISTRO**
AT: K VILLAGE
93-95 Sukhumvit Soi 26 Sukhumvit ⑦
+66 (0)2 661 3942

Wine Connection is successful due to its simple formula of joining a wine shop with a cosy deli and bistro that serves up great comfort food. The bottles of wine get served at retail prices, and the pizza, pasta, and make-your-own cheese platters won't break the bank, making it a bargain compared to having a bottle of vino elsewhere.

182 **WINE I LOVE YOU**
AT: THE EMQUARTIER
637 Sukhumvit Road Sukhumvit ⑦
+66 (0)2 003 6213
www.wineiloveyou.com

While the setting may be in Bangkok's glitziest mall, the focus here is on reasonably priced food, ranging from Thai to fish and chips, that pair up with good deals on average wines. The place is always crowded with young Thais, and you'll come here for the vibe and price rather than the selection.

183 RIEDEL WINE BAR & CELLAR

AT: GAYSORN VILLAGE, 2ND FLOOR

999 Ploenchit Road
Pathumwan ①
+66 (0)2 656 1133
www.riedelwinebarbkk.com

Tucked away in the snazzy Gaysorn Village mall, Riedel has an excellent selection of fine wines ranging from Old to New World, along with a selection of organic and artisan wines from around the globe. Prices reflect the high rents here, but you can opt for the tapas and tasting menus which offer appetisers along with several glasses of wine.

184 WINE PUB PULLMAN

AT: PULLMAN BANGKOK KING POWER

8-2 Rangnam Road
Northern Bangkok ⑪
+66 (0)2 680 9999
www.winepubbangkok.com

With 48 wines by the glass available, and over 130 by the bottle, this is Bangkok's most extensive wine bar. The bar features a Vinoteca wine machine, which preserves bottle flavour once you've opened one, and there is also a 2-star Michelin chef presiding over the French bistro and tapas offerings to go with the fine wines.

185 NO IDEA

8/3-4 Sukhumvit Soi 22
Sukhumvit ⑦
+66 (0)2 663 6686
www.noideabkk.com

This cafe and gastropub is noted for its burgers and steaks, but even better is its extensive wine selection. Only a few are available by the glass, but there are over 100 interesting bottles to choose from, ranging from French and Italian to Chilean and Australian. The casual vibe is popular with those seeking a decent meal followed by relaxed drinking without paying 5-star prices.

JIM THOMPSON

60 PLACES TO SHOP

The 5 most interesting
MARKETS

---

186 CHATUCHAK WEEKEND MARKET

587/10 Kamphaeng Phet 2 Road
Northern Bangkok ⑪
www.chatuchakmarket.org

Known as the 'mother of all markets', Chatuchak, affectionately called JJ by locals, is a sprawling everything-under-the-sun affair, from pets to vintage clothing, furniture, plants, and more. There are over 15.000 booths here, with more than 200.000 visitors packing it in each Saturday and Sunday.

187 ASIATIQUE THE RIVERFRONT

2194 Charoenkrung Road
Southern Bangkok ⑬
+66 (0)2 108 4488
www.asiatique thailand.com

Set on the banks of the Chao Phraya, this lively night spot has over 1500 boutique shops and restaurants set in four old warehouses themed to evoke the river trade here in the early 1900s. In addition to the shopping, there's a ladyboy cabaret and traditional Thai puppet theatre, plus Bangkok's largest ferris wheel.

188 KHLONG TOEI WET MARKET

Cnr. of Rama IV Road and Ratchadapisek Road
Eastern Bangkok ⑫⑦
+66 (0)2 350 1228

No visit to Bangkok is complete without a trip to a traditional 'wet' produce market, and Khlong Toei is one of the best: a sprawling affair where produce and seafood get unloaded in the wee hours of the morning, with the market being thronged by local shoppers come sunrise.

189 BANGKOK FARMERS' MARKET
AT: GATEWAY EKAMAI
982/22 Sukhumvit Road
Thonglor/Ekkamai ⑧
+66 (0)92 257 1106
www.bkkfm.org

The weekend farmers' market gives Bangkok a more communal and European vibe than usual. Starting as just a small collection of entrepreneurs, it has grown to a successful place to not only buy organic produce, homebaked bread and pastries, and local crafts, but a place to bring the family and hang around, with a host of interesting vendors and mellow vibe.

190 PAK KHLONG TALAD
225 Chakphet Road
Rattanakosin Island ③
+66 (0)2 223 2377

Bangkok's flower market is far more of a working market than a tourist attraction, partly because the main excitement of the market, the arrival and unloading of all the flowers from all over the country, occurs around 2 to 3 am, but it can still be enjoyed by day, with bouquets piled high and plenty of trading.

186 CHATUCHAK WEEKEND MARKET

5 nice places to
BUY SILK

191 ALMETA SILK

20/3 Sukhumvit Soi 23
Sukhumvit ⑦
+66 (0)2 204 1413
www.almeta.com

Almeta have a proven track record making high quality Thai silk, and even have a 'Lazy Silk', the only machine washable silk, as part of their product line. Their cosy shop features over 1000 different types of silk colours, yarn types, and various weights up to 12-ply, and they sell custom-made bedding, cushions, and clothing.

192 JIM THOMPSON

6 Soi Kasemsan 2,
Rama I Road
Pathumwan ①
+66 (0)2 216 7368
www.jimthompson.com

Jim Thompson brought Thai silk to the rest of the world, making it world-famous in the 1950s. Today, his beautiful traditional teak house is a museum and home to one of the many Jim Thompson silk outlets. You can tour the old home, learn about Thai silk, and then buy some souvenirs.

193 NAJ COLLECTION

42 Convent Road
Silom ②
+66 (0)2 632 1004
www.najcollection.com

Naj Collection is an old-school shop, part of the elegant Naj Cuisine restaurant, specialising in glamorous high end handmade silk products. You can find superb silk souvenirs here, ranging from home decor pieces to accessories. An added plus is the beautiful old teak building the shop and restaurant are housed in.

194 T. SHINAWATRA SILK

94 Sukhumvit Soi 23
Sukhumvit ⑦
+66 (0)2 258 0295
www.tshinawatra.com

In a town where ascertaining genuine quality can be dubious if you don't know your silks, Shinawatra is rivalled only by Jim Thompson when it comes to quality and expertise. Founded in 1929, it is Thailand's oldest silk establishment. Scarves, cushion covers, and a variety of bags are just a sample of the fine wares.

195 QUEEN THAI SILK
AT: TRENDY PLAZA

10/4 Sukhumvit Soi 13
Sukhumvit ⑦
+66 (0)2 651 0082

Women will want to shop here if interested in getting custom-made silk dresses and other women's clothing. The shop relocated from their former branch around the corner near Soi 15, so make sure your map shows the updated address. You'll be custom-measured and fitted, and have a wide choice of different quality fabrics.

192 JIM THOMPSON

5 of the best
TAILORS

196 TAILOR ON TEN
93 Sukhumvit Soi 8
Sukhumvit ⑦
+66 (0)84 877 1543
www.tailoronten.com

Owned and operated by two Canadian brothers, this shop is praised for honesty and personal service in a city where tailors can come a scam a dozen. The brothers hand-pick every thread and button, the tailoring is done in-house, and the quality is guaranteed. The assured workmanship brings in every type of traveller and local.

197 NARRY TAILOR
155/22 Sukhumvit
Soi 11/1
Sukhumvit ⑦
+66 (0)81 919 2533
www.narry.com

Bangkok is famed for its Indian tailors, who can make custom-fitted shirts, slacks, suits, and tuxedos at great cost for quality. While you can find cheaper, you tend to get what you pay for here, and Narry is a bespoke tailor who has been receiving accolades for a superior level of workmanship, quality, and service.

198 PINKY TAILOR
AT: MAHATUN PLAZA ARCADE
888/40 Ploenchit Road
Pathumwan ①
+66 (0)2 253 6328
www.pinkytailor.com

Pinky has been around since 1980 and has a legion of local followers. Mr. Pinky and his son serve both men and women, with skirts, shirts, suits, and uniforms just part of their stock. Customers are measured both for each garment and the cloth needed for it to be cut.

199 SIAM EMPORIUM

390/2-3 Sukhumvit Road
Sukhumvit ⑦
+66 (0)2 663 4809
www.siamemporium
tailors.com

This bespoke Indian tailor has been around since 1976, with years of experience in the fashion industry, which sets them apart from the other line-up of tailors that can be found as you walk down the row of shops on lower Sukhumvit. The other tailors tend to have guys outside trying to lure you in, but Siam Emporium relies on their expertise and track record instead.

200 BUTTON UP

113/6 Sukhumvit Soi 55
(near Thonglor Soi 5)
Thonglor ⑧
+66 (0)2 712 6111
www.thebuttonup.com

Rapper Snoop Dogg had his threads done here, plenty of Thai celebrities stop in, and the customised service and fitting is the best in Bangkok. You'll pay high prices here, but you'll get Loro Piana and other fine European fabrics for your suit.

200 BUTTON UP

5 fun
STREET MARKETS

---

201 PRATUNAM

869/15 Ratchaprarop
Road (Petchaburi
Intersection)
Pathumwan ①

Pratunam is known for cheap wholesale clothing, shoes, and accessories, not as cheap as Bo Bae, but here you can also buy individual pieces rather than only in bulk. There are thousands of stalls crammed into the lanes between Petchaburi Road and the Baiyoke II Tower.

202 BO BAE
AT: BOBAE TOWER

488 Damrongrak Road
Rattanakosin Island ③
+66 (0)2 628 1888

Locals in the know come here for the best prices if they want to buy in bulk. T-shirts, pants, textiles, and jewellery, it's all here, at a fraction of what they cost around the rest of town. The market is both inside the Bobae Tower, as well as outside along the canal.

203 SAMPENG

Sampeng Lane,
Soi Wanit 1
Chinatown ④

Also called Sampeng Lane, as the market is inside a narrow alley running the length of Chinatown, you can find clothing, fabrics, electronics, shoes, cosmetics, and pretty much everything here, and if you buy 10 items or more, you'll get incredible deals. It's a vintage Bangkok experience, but be prepared for intense crowds.

204 KHLONG SAN

38 Charoen Nakhon
Road
Khlong San
Thonburi ⑤

Aimed at teen to 22 year old females, the market might not appear much on first glance – mostly jeans, tops, short shorts, and copied fashion accessories – it nevertheless offers a glimpse of Thai youth culture, and if you come over here at night, there is lots of cheap local food and even bands playing.

205 WANG LANG

Trok Wang Lang,
Wang Lang Road
Thonburi ⑤ ③

This busy street market is noted for authentic Thai food and traditional snacks. It sits on the Thonburi side of the river, and it serves the entire staff of Siriraj Hospital behind it, as well as masses of Thammasat University students, who hop on the three baht cross river ferry to come over here and snack.

201 PRATUNAM

5

MALLS *where you can find everything you need*

───────

206 SIAM PARAGON

991 Rama I Road
Pathumwan ①
+66 (0)2 610 8000
www.siamparagon.co.th

Many consider Siam Paragon to be the granddaddy of all malls and the epicentre of Bangkok. Both the elite and the masses shop here, and you'll find everything from Gucci, Louis Vuitton, and Georgio Armani shops to a 15-screen multiplex cinema, an IMAX theatre, an Ocean World aquarium, a gourmet market, and hundreds of restaurants.

207 EMQUARTIER

637 Sukhumvit Road
Sukhumvit ⑦
+66 (0)2 269 1000
www.theemdistrict.com

This is the latest addition to Bangkok's upscale shopping. EmQuartier has flagship stores from Valentino, MCM, Jimmy Choo and a massive collection of high-end boutique shops. The mall also boasts Asia's largest man-made waterfall, a world class Virgin fitness centre, an IMAX theatre, and a tropical garden zone.

208 TERMINAL 21

88 Sukhumvit Soi 19
Sukhumvit ⑦
+66 (0)2 108 0888
www.terminal21.co.th

Terminal 21 isn't as glitzy as some of the other showcase malls, but is a tourist favourite due to its design: each floor is named and themed after a tourist-popular world location.

209 **CENTRALWORLD**
999/9 Rama I Road
Pathumwan ①
+66 (0)2 021 9999
www.centralworld.co.th

CentralWorld is a mall of superlatives. Largest in Bangkok and Thailand, the sixth largest mall in the world, 550.000 square metres of retail space, and so forth. Fifteen cinemas, an ice-skating rink, kids' zone, sky bar, hotel, and even outdoor beer gardens in the winter months, all located smack in the centre of the city.

210 **CENTRAL EMBASSY**
1031 Ploenchit Road
Pathumwan ①
+66 (0)2 119 7777
www.centralembassy.com

Central Embassy is one of Bangkok's newest malls, very upscale, and featuring an architecturally striking façade and curved glittering cover. It is home to Bangkok's most elegant movie theatre, along with a great array of fine places to eat, and the whole 6th floor is an open space art bookshop surrounded by cool cafes and eateries.

207 EMQUARTIER

The 5 best
THAI CLOTHING DESIGNERS

---

211 SENADA THEORY
AT: SIAM CENTER, 3RD FLOOR
979 Rama I Road
Pathumwan ⓘ
+66 (0)2 252 2757
www.senadatheory.com

Senada combines Thai silks and Indian embroidery to create fashionable clothing for women. The melange of ethnic, eclectic and modern are both feminist and cutting edge. Senada is at the forefront of Thai design. The Siam Center flagship store has the best selection of their catalogue.

212 DISAYA
AT: CENTRALWORLD, GROOVE ZONE, 2ND FLOOR
999/9 Rama I Road
Pathumwan ⓘ
+66 (0)2 646 1828
www.disaya.com

Showing off her stint at St. Martin's Fashion College in London, Disaya mixes Thai cuteness with British practicality, and celebrities such as Jennifer Lopez and Amy Winehouse have worn her fun cartoon print dresses. Her boutique store in Central Groove has 120 square metres of pink and gold tones to accent all the chic clothing.

213 SRETSIS
AT: CENTRAL EMBASSY, 2ND FLOOR
1031 Ploenchit Road
Pathumwan ⓘ
+66 (0)2 160 5874
www.sretsis.com

The name means 'sisters' spelled backwards, and is the now renowned brand created by three Thai sisters who were influenced by their New York and Paris fashion design school and haute couture internship experiences. They create girlie graphic print clothing that mixes a retro look with modern twists.

214 FLYNOW BY CHAMNAN
AT: SIAM PARAGON, 1ST FLOOR

991 Rama I Road
Pathumwan ①
+66 (0)2 610 9410
www.flynowbangkok.com

Bangkok's Harper's Bazaar Fashion Director and haute couturier Chamnan Pakdeesuk is the longest-standing success story on the Bangkok design scene. Starting with a tiny ladies' wear collection, Flynow has evolved into an avant-garde label, acclaimed as a top designer at London Fashion Week, and today has expanded into leather, accessories, and much more.

215 GREYHOUND
AT: SIAM CENTER, 1ST FLOOR

979 Rama I Road
Pathumwan ①
+66 (0)2 251 4917
www.greyhound.co.th

What is now one of the city's top fashion teams was started in 1980 by four friends with no fashion design background. They started out with t-shirts for men, and now have a long line of both men's and women's wear which tries to blend modernism and minimalism, with the clothing suitable for both formal and casual situations, perfect for the tropics.

211 SENADA THEORY

The 5 most interesting
BOOKSHOPS

---

216 **DASA BOOK CAFE**
714/4 Sukhumvit Road
(betw Soi 26-28)
Sukhumvit ⑦
+66 (0)2 661 2993
www.dasabookcafe.com

This quaint small town-style used books store is a haven for bibliophiles and has Bangkok's best selection of used books. Plenty of current titles, guidebooks, and harder to find novels feature as well. The store buys back their own books at 50%, all titles are in a well categorised data base.

217 **KINOKUNIYA**
AT: EMQUARTIER, 3RD FLOOR
689 Sukhumvit Road
Sukhumvit ⑦
+66 (0)2 003 6507
www.thailand.
kinokuniya.com

The large Japanese chain has several branches in Bangkok malls, and has the largest selection of English titles in town, not to mention titles in Japanese, Chinese, and Thai as well. From maps to travel guides to bestsellers, everything is clearly labelled, the stores are extremely spacious, and you can order books as well.

218 **PASSPORT BOOKSHOP**
523 Pra Sumen Road
Rattanakosin Island ③
+66 (0)2 629 0694

Jazz music and cappuccino greet you at this artsy and cosy shop in Bangkok's old town. The focus is on travel titles, spirituality, and Buddhism, all favourites of the travelling owner, and there is a mix of Thai titles and English. With its cafe seating, it's an excellent place to linger.

219 OPEN HOUSE BOOKS
AT: CENTRAL EMBASSY, 6TH FLOOR

1031 Ploenchit Road
Pathumwan ①
+66 (0)2 119 7777

This beautiful new open-plan bookstore at the top of the suave Central Embassy Mall features a vast collection of art books, plus couches to read on, co-working spaces, and an array of eateries surrounding the books, meaning you can munch, read, and relax all at the same time.

220 CANDIDE
AT: THE JAM FACTORY

41/1 Charoen Nakhon Road
Thonburi ⑤
+66 (0)2 861 0967
www.candidebooks.com

Only a few classics like Hemingway or Mark Twain are in English here, but it is still worth visiting. The bookstore sits inside the Jam Factory, a collection of artsy shops, restaurants, and cafes on the Chao Phraya River. Famed Thai architect Duangrit Bunnag is the owner of Candide, and his industrial minimalist vibe complements the excellent cafe and hangout space.

219 OPEN HOUSE BOOKS

The 5 best
THAI PRODUCT SHOPS

221 **PAYA SHOP**
203 Thonglor Soi 10
Thonglor/Ekkamai ⑧
+66 (0)2 711 4457
www.payashop.net

Owners Pramort and his wife Jeab have been involved with village crafts, textiles, and local artisans all their lives, and their shop has made-to-order handmade textiles, traditional furniture, and homemade artisanal crafts. You'll get plenty of personalised attention here, and it's a great place for souvenir shopping.

222 **TR GIFT SHOP**
2-4 Charoen Krung Soi 40
Silom/Bang Rak ②
+66 (0)2 234 5773
www.trgiftshop.
blogspot.com

This family-run gift shop specialises in cutlery and stainless steel bowls, plates, and other kitchenware. This is the place to go if you are looking for kitchen items, from serving dishes to bamboo-patterned flatware and water pitchers or salt and pepper shakers to take home. You'll also find some silver items and other jewellery downstairs.

223 **NARAI PHAND**
AT: PRESIDENT TOWER, G/F
973 Ploenchit Road
Pathumwan ①
+66 (0)2 656 0398
www.naraiphand.com

One of Bangkok's oldest handicraft sellers, this elegant warehouse-like shop is noted for its collection of fine Benjarong ceramics, along with pewter, lacquerware, bronze, and celadon pieces. You can find teak wood statues, silk scarves, and just about any authentic Thai curio here.

224 THAI CRAFT FAIR

35 Bamrung Muang
Road
Rattanakosin Island ③
+66 (0)2 221 1330
www.thaicraft.org

Thai Craft sells a range of village-made artisan items, from soaps and spa products to food and home decor. You'll find silver from the Karen hill tribe here next to water hyacinth baskets from Isaan, and all the products are focused on fair trade and sustainable development for rural regions in Thailand. The shop also runs a monthly craft fair in the Jasmine Building on Sukhumvit Road.

225 OTOP THE GALLERY

Ploenchit-Sukhumvit
(expressway entrance)
Pathumwan ⑦
+66 (0)2 650 8007
www.thaitambon.com/
otop

OTOP shops are part of an entrepreneurial program showcasing and supporting local products from each tambon (sub-district) in every province in Thailand. You'll find hill tribe jewelry from the north, silks from Isaan, pottery from Koh Kret, batik and carved wood from the south, plus spices, regional food products, clothes, shoes, and tons more.

5 great shops for
R E T R O *lovers*

---

226 **(UN)FASHION**

3 Ekkamai Soi 10
Thonglor/Ekkamai ⑧
+66 (0)2 726 9592

As Bangkok falls more and more in love with retro, this shop is super popular with Thais for its collection of vintage shoes, boots, bags, and leather items imported from Europe, the U.S., and Japan. The Japanese and Thai owners also run a cute cafe out back, making it a great stop for some retro footwear and a snack.

227 **PAPAYA VINTAGE**

306/1 Lad Phrao 55/2
Northern Bangkok ⑪
+66 (0)2 539 8220
www.papaya55.com

It is worth coming here just as a tourist attraction. This sprawling warehouse is packed from floor to ceiling with an incredible array of vintage collectibles, toys, retro furniture, and other bric-à-brac so eclectic that it defies description. There are life-size Ultraman figures, birdcages, LP players, neon signs, and claw bathtubs. Nothing is labelled, nor priced, nor is there any order to any of it.

228 AGAIN & AGAIN

150/1-9 Market Place,
Thonglor Soi 4
Thonglor/Ekkamai ⑧
+66 (0)86 626 6965
www.vintage
againandagain.com

The owner, Masiri Tamsakul, is a former stylist at Marie Claire, and she personally selects all the colourful vintage clothing here on overseas buying trips in Japan, the U.S., and Europe. You'll find a selection of colourful mostly women's clothing and dress up costume jewellery, and Ms. Tamsakul keeps a rotating and plentiful stock.

229 WOODEN SUBMARINE

121/118 Phaya Thai Road
Pathumwan ①
+66 (0)81 255 2866

Wooden Submarine hosts an excellent collection of vintage Americana. The shop features lots of clothing from the U.S. ranging from the 1920s to the 1970s. You'll find army fatigues, uniform jackets, firefighters' jumpsuits, and other eccentricities of another era.

230 8 MUSIQUE

AT: EI8HT BUILDING
88/36 Sukhumvit Soi 55
Thonglor/Ekkamai ⑧
+66 (0)2 713 8366

The LP lives on at Bangkok's best vintage music shop. The owners keep the love of vinyl alive, with copies of the classics like The Beatles and Pink Floyd, plus a huge array of indie titles. You'll easily find 1950s Chet Baker jazz selections as well as 80s classic rock.

5 shops for
THAI ANTIQUES
and HANDICRAFTS

---

231 RIVER CITY

23 Trok
Rongnamkhaeng, Si
Phaya Pier, Yota Road
Silom/Bang Rak ②
+66 (0)2 237 0077
www.rivercitybangkok.com

River City is an entire mall filled with shops that specialise in fine art and antiques. It's one of Bangkok's longest running antique houses and originally served as an antique auction house. The first Saturday of every month still sees the 50+ shops here involved with a large antique auction. Shop owners here are some of Bangkok's pioneers of the antique trade.

232 SILOM GALLERIA
AT: JEWELRY TRADE CENTER
BUILDING, 25TH FLOOR
919/1 Silom Road
Silom/Bang Rak ②
+66 (0)2 630 0944

Set in the Jewelry Trade Center, this is a great spot for buying antiques and jewellery. You'll find jewellery and crafts shops in the basement, selling from fine Chinese porcelain to brass, and the rest of the floors have been converted to art gallery displays, with exhibitions and paintings for sale.

233 HOUSE OF CHAO
9/1 Decho Road
Silom/Bang Rak ②
+66 (0)2 635 7188

It's worth a visit just to gape at the three-storey colonial mansion the shop is housed in, and the treasures inside, which, most appropriately, all come from the home's past, and include old clocks, teak furniture, chandeliers, and other items to outfit a bygone era manor.

234 O.P. PLACE
30/1 Charoen Krung
Soi 38
Silom/Bang Rak ②
+66 (0)2 266 0186
www.opthai.com/opplace

This elegant colonial heritage building near the French Embassy holds a treasure trove of high end fine arts and antiques. Shops here sell Middle Eastern carpets, rare antiques, premium leather goods, and top Thai silks. If you've got the money, this is the place to spend it for quality trinkets.

235 PAUL'S ANTIQUES
50 Sukhumvit Soi 13
Sukhumvit ⑦
+66 (0)2 253 9025
www.paulsantiques.com

An American expat who loved Burmese colonial teak pieces built up this wonderfully eclectic antique furniture shop, and it is now run by Thai-American Angela Somwaiya, who combs flea markets and off-the-beaten track locales in Southeast Asia to add to the collection of golden teak chairs, tables, and wedding sets.

The 5 best
NIGHT MARKETS

---

236 SRINAKARIN TRAIN MARKET (TALAD ROT FAI)
Srinakarin Soi 51
Eastern Bangkok ⑫
+66 (0)81 827 5885

While retro furniture, antiques, and vintage hot rod cars are the highlight of this sprawling outdoor antique and retro market, you can buy just about anything here, from clothing and old records to sewing machines, and there are also some very cool cafes and bars to hang out in with the young hipsters.

237 PATPONG NIGHT MARKET
Patpong Soi 2, Silom Road
Silom/Bang Rak ②

Certainly unique in that you are shopping amongst souvenir stalls surrounded by go go bars, perhaps Patpong's fame is due more to what's in the background. Nevertheless, for a collection of typical cheap souvenirs, from cushion covers to fisherman-pants, tourists love after-dinner strolls here. Just make sure to bargain hard and know that the watches are fake.

238 TALAD NEON
1087 Petchaburi Road
Pathumwan ①

While not as hip or atmospheric as the other main night markets, the location is great, right downtown in the Pratunam market zone. You can continue your shopping here with a decent collection of Thai souvenirs, get a haircut or massage, drink at a VW cocktail bar, and even play bingo.

239 JJ GREEN

1 Kampaeng Phet 3
Road, Chatuchak
Northern Bangkok ⑪
+66 (0)62 461 5951
www.jjgreen.com

Formerly called the Siam Gypsy Market, this outdoor night market is a cooler (both in weather and vibe) experience than nearby Chatuchak, as there is more space and greenery, and fewer crowds. The market features a mix of retro vendors and plenty of small happening bars that have live music playing on weekends.

240 RATCHADA TRAIN MARKET

Ratchadapisek Road
(next to Esplanade)
Northern Bangkok ⑪
+66 (0)92 713 5599

Noted for great live music, this second version of the popular train market focuses also on retro furnishings, cars and motorcycles, and clothing. Given that this area of Ratchada Road is home to lots of university students, young folk's clubs, and is a lower-rent neighbourhood, this market has a young and energetic vibe.

236 TALAD ROT FAI

The 5 best
ELECTRONICS
shops

---

241 PANTIP PLAZA

604/3 Petchaburi Road
Pathumwan ⓘ
+66 (0)2 252 9933
www.pantipplaza.com

Pantip used to be synonymous with pirated X-rated movies, and while they still have some upstairs, the place has been given a facelift and is a good spot for just about anything electronic. From computers to cameras and phones, there is a huge selection. The further back you walk, the more you'll find specialised shops with used parts and hard to find pieces that you won't get anywhere else.

242 MAHBOONKRONG (MBK)

444 Phayathai Road
Pathumwan ⓘ
+66 (0)2 620 9000
www.mbk-center.co.th

MBK is filled with an insane number of smartphone sellers on the 4th floor, but if you want the latest Samsung, better buy from their main shop here, not from the tiny stalls. You can unlock your phone here, pick up any gadget for it, and the Fotofile camera shops on the 1st and 4th floors here are some of the most reputable in Bangkok.

243 KHLONG THOM MARKET

499 Worachak Road
Chinatown ④
+66 (0)2 222 1100
www.klongthom.co.th

One man's junk is another's treasure at this market located in the bowels of Chinatown. It used to be known as the 'flashlight market' due to the need for customers to use flashlights after dark to discern whether or not the goods they were buying were of decent quality. While many of the electronic wares you may find here might be of dubious make, there are also a few gems.

244 SEACON SQUARE IT CITY

AT: SEACON SQUARE,
1ST FLOOR
Srinakarin Soi 51
Eastern Bangkok ⑫
+66 (0)2 721 8484
www.itcity.co.th

The latest desktops, laptops, smartphones, and all computer and phone gear and gadgets can be found here. It's well outside the city centre, but you can come here to shop and stop in at the Talad Rot Fai retro market for drinks afterwards.

245 FORTUNE TOWN

Cnr. of Rama IX Road
and Ratchadaphisek
Road
Northern Bangkok ⑪
+66 (0)2 248 5855
www.fortunetown.co.th

You'll find a large selection of phones and phone related gadgets, televisions, monitors, computers, and cameras at Fortune Town, with prices pretty similar to Pantip Plaza and MBK, maybe even cheaper, as it's mostly a Thai clientele here.

BAIYOKE II TOWER

20 BUILDINGS AND MONUMENTS TO ADMIRE

5

ICONIC
buildings

---

246 **HUA LAMPHONG STATION**
Khwaeng Rong Muang
Chinatown ④
+66 (0)2 223 3762
www.thairailways.com/
train-station.bangkok.html

Bangkok's main railway station was constructed in 1916, and features ornate Neo-Renaissance Italian architecture, with large stained glass windows and a soaring semi-circular interior. With a grand new rail terminus set to open outside the city in a few years, Hua Lamphong will eventually be turned into a railway museum and preserved as a classic.

247 **MAHANAKHON TOWER**
114 Narathiwat Road
Sathorn ⑥
+66 (0)2 234 1414
www.mahanakhon.com

This is Bangkok's new tallest building, opened in 2016, standing some 314 metres in height. Its unique design resembles a prism, and it has a pixelated look, visible from almost everywhere in Bangkok. There are plans to open an observatory at the top of it.

248 **BAIYOKE II TOWER**
222 Ratchaprarop Road
Pathumwan ①
+66 (0)2 656 3000
www.baiyokehotel.com

Until recently (see MahaNakhon Tower above), Baiyoke II was the tallest building in Bangkok, at 309 metres, and it's one of the tallest hotel buildings in the world. You can access the 84th floor rooftop observatory, which rotates and offers a dizzying panorama of the sea of skyscrapers all around.

249 **SUVARNABHUMI AIRPORT**
999 Moo 1, Bangna-Trad
Road, Bang Phli
Eastern Bangkok ⑫
+66 (0)2 132 1888
www.suvarnabhumi
airport.com

Meaning 'golden land', venerating
an ancient Buddhist kingdom, the
cantilevered roof domes of Suvarnabhumi
were constructed to look like floating
waves, and are quite impressive viewed
upon arrival into the airport. This is
a remarkable piece of architecture,
especially considering that it has been
built on what was a real swamp.

250 **THE ROBOT BUILDING**
(UOB BANK BUILDING)
19 South Sathorn Road
Sathorn ⑥
+66 (0)2 343 3000
www.uob.co.th

Home to the UOB Bank headquarters,
this building looks like a robot, with eyes,
ears, and a body. It was designed by noted
Thai architect Sumet Jumsai, who was
asked to make something promoting the
computer-age of banking. The structure is
also Jumsai's rebuttal to the post-modern
architecture that has dominated Bangkok.

246 **HUA LAMPHONG STATION**

The 5 most
IMPORTANT
MONUMENTS

---

251 DEMOCRACY MONUMENT
Ratchadamnoen Klang
Road, Khwaeng Wat
Bowon Niwet
Rattanakosin Island ③

This 1939 monument remembers the Siam
Revolution of 1932, when Thailand became
a constitutional monarchy. The towering
'wings' were designed by an Italian sculptor and the monument sits in the centre
of traffic-heavy Rachadamnoen Road. It
is most atmospheric at sunset and in the
evening when lit up.

252 THE GIANT SWING
Bamrung Muang Road,
Khwaeng Sao Chingcha
Rattanakosin Island ③

Called 'Saochingcha' in Thai, this towering
21-metre swing dates from 1784, although
it has since been reconstructed. It was used
for Brahmin religious ceremonies where
men actually rode it, trying to reach for
bags of silver placed beneath it while in
full motion. It remains one of Bangkok's
most iconic sights today.

253 VICTORY MONUMENT
Phaya Thai Road
Northern Bangkok ⑩

Victory Monument, erected in 1941 to
celebrate the Thai victory over French
colonial powers in Indochina, features a
tall obelisk and a set of statues depicting
heroic soldiers. Today the monument is
known for being the centre of Bangkok's
largest traffic hub in the evenings.

254 CHINATOWN ARCH

322 Tri Mit Road
Chinatown ④

Also known as Chinatown Gate or Odeon Circle, this arch was built in 1999 to celebrate former King Bhumibol's 72nd birthday. It is decorated with calligraphy in Chinese reading 'Long live the King'. It is seen as the entryway into Bangkok's large Chinatown, and is the focal point of Chinese New Year celebrations.

255 OCTOBER 14 MEMORIAL

Soi Damnoen Klang Tai,
Khwaeng Wat Bowon
Niwet
Rattanakosin Island ③

This amphitheatre monument pays somber remembrance to demonstrators that were killed by the military during a peaceful demonstration against the military government in 1973. Half a million protestors had lined Rachadamnoen Road, and 77 students and civilians were killed when troops opened fire. The protests marked the beginning of the end of the military-led government at the time.

251 DEMOCRACY MONUMENT

5 buildings used by
ROYALTY

256 **ANANTA SAMAKHOM THRONE HALL**
U Thong Nai Road
Dusit ⑩
+66 (0)2 283 9411
www.artsofthekingdom.com

This regal domed marble palace was completed in 1915 and was a reception hall for King Rama VI and then used for state functions and served as the House of Parliament until 1974. It's now a museum featuring outstanding Italian Renaissance architecture and art.

257 **CHITRALADA ROYAL VILLA**
AT: DUSIT PALACE
Suan Chitlada
Dusit ⑩
+66 (0)2 281 1847
www.kanchanapisek.or.th

The Chitralada Villa is part of the sprawling Dusit Palace complex, and was the official residence of Thai's reigning king, Bhumibol Adulyadej, when he was in Bangkok. The palace isn't open to the public and is far less grand than other Bangkok royal residences.

258 **PHAYA THAI PALACE**
315 Ratchawithi Road
Dusit ⑩
+66 (0)2 354 7987
www.phyathaipalace.org

Another one of King Rama V's private residences, this Sino-Portuguese-styled manor, complete with frescoes and Byzantine architecture, became a luxury hotel and was later used as a military hospital. Today it is still military property, but has been turned into a museum that is open to the public.

259 VIMANMEK PALACE

16 Rajawithi Road
Dusit ⑩
+66 (0)2 628 6300
www.palaces.thai.net

This stunning Victorian teak mansion was built at the start of the 1900s and used by King Rama V as a palace. It later became one of Bangkok's most popular museums, but recently has been closed to the public.

260 SUAN PAKKAD PALACE

352-354 Sri Ayutthaya Road
Dusit ⑩
+66 (0)2 245 4934
www.suanpakkad.com

These eight ornate teak houses were home to the royal Prince and Princess Chumbhot. They were built in 1952 as their private residence, but some 35 years later, they turned it into a public museum. It is a tranquil oasis in Bangkok, with the beautiful old homes overlooking a lush garden.

256 ANANTA SAMAKHOM THRONE HALL

5

COLONIAL

buildings to appreciate

---

261 **THE EAST ASIATIC COMPANY**
Charoen Krung Soi 40, Oriental Pier
Silom/Bang Rak ②

This fading Venetian building is a colonial gem, built by the Danish East Asiatic Company to handle its Far East sea freight trade routes at the beginning of 1900 and to connect Thailand to Europe. The building is still in use and its façade can be photographed from the Oriental Pier.

262 **OLD CUSTOMS HOUSE**
37 Charoen Krung Soi 36
Silom/Bang Rak ②

The Customs House dates from 1880, and used to levy tariffs on ships sailing up and down the Chao Phraya. These days, it is falling into disrepair, but it is still quite atmospheric. In its prime, it rivalled the East Asiatic Building. You may have seen it at its best in Wong Kar Wai's film *In the Mood for Love*.

263 **ASSUMPTION CATHEDRAL**
23 Charoen Krung Soi 40
Silom/Bang Rak ②
+66 (0)2 234 8556
www.assumption-cathedral.com

A red brick building built in Renaissance style, Assumption dates from 1909. It is the most important Catholic building in Thailand. The Romanesque twin towers are home to Sunday mass in English at 10 am. There is also a convent and college adjacent to the premises.

264 **MINISTRY OF DEFENCE**
Lak Muang, Khwaeng
Phra Borom Maha
Ratchawang
Rattanakosin Island ③
+66(0)2 223 2837

The neoclassical golden building dates from the 1880s and faces the Grand Palace. It is kept in great shape and the exterior features gaily painted green shutters contrasting with a bright yellow facade. Guards sometimes bar access to the side streets around it, but you can take photos of the building without problem.

265 **THE HOUSE ON SATHORN**
106 North Sathorn Road
Sathorn ⑥
+66 (0)2 344 4025
*www.thehouse
onsathorn.com*

This beautiful building was formerly the home of Lord Sathorn, who built the Sathorn Canal and then built this mansion in 1889. It later became the luxury Hotel Royal, the Embassy of the Soviet Union, and then of the Russian Federation. It now serves as an elegant restaurant and bar under the auspices of the W Hotel.

265 THE HOUSE ON SATHORN

ERAWAN SHRINE

50 PLACES TO DISCOVER BANGKOK

The 5 most interesting
TEMPLES

266 **WAT TRAIMIT**

661 Charoen Krung
Road
Chinatown ④
+66 (0)89 002 2700
www.wattraimitr-
withayaram.com

This ornate temple is the jewel of Chinatown and contains the largest pure gold statue in the world, a 5,5 ton Buddha image, which is the prime reason for visiting the temple. There is also an excellent museum of Chinese-Thai heritage on the premises.

267 **WAT ARUN**
AKA: THE TEMPLE OF DAWN

158 Wang Doem Road
Thonburi ⑤
+66 (0)2 891 2185
www.watarun.net

Known as the Temple of the Golden Dawn, Wat Arun is one of Bangkok's most iconic landmarks. Named after the Indian god of dawn, the Khmer style tower stands proudly above the Chao Phraya River, and is at its best when lit up by the early rays of the sun. The best views of it are from across the river.

268 **SRI MAHA MARIAMMAN**

Cnr. of Silom Road and
Pan Road
Silom/Bang Rak ②
+66 (0)2 238 4007

Also known as Wat Khaek, this is the most important Hindu temple in Bangkok, and also its most colourful one, with a façade of hundreds of deities all done up in a riot of colours. Built in the 1860s, the temple is at its best during the Navaratri festival each October, thronged by thousands of devotees.

266 **WAT TRAIMIT**

267 **WAT ARUN**

270 **WAT PHO**

269 **WAT PHRA KAEW**
AKA: THE TEMPLE OF THE
EMERALD BUDDHA
AT: THE GRAND PALACE
Na Phra Lan Road
Rattanakosin Island ③
+66 (0)2 623 5500
www.palaces.thai.net

Housed inside The Grand Palace, the temple contains a solid jade Buddha, which may only be touched by the king. It is probably the most revered spiritual image in the entire country. Pilgrims flock here to pray and pay respects. Do note that Thais come here for serious worship and that it is far more than a tourist attraction, but it is worth coming on weekends just to check out the pilgrimage crowds.

270 **WAT PHO**
2 Sanam Chai Road
Rattanakosin Island ③
+66 (0)2 226 0335
www.watpho.com

This is Bangkok's oldest and biggest temple, noted for its 50-metre massive reclining golden Buddha statue. This is a colossal piece of art, with the giant feet containing 108 auspicious Buddha signs inlaid in mother of pearl. Additionally, the traditional massage school here has the reputation for being one of Thailand's best.

The 5 most important
S H R I N E S
to visit

---

271 **LAKSHMI SHRINE**
AT: GAYSORN PLAZA,
4TH FLOOR
999 Phloenchit Road
Pathumwan ⓘ

By far the most beautiful of all Bangkok shrines. The small statue of Lakshmi hides up on the roof of Gaysorn Plaza. From here, the goddess of wealth, prosperity, and fortune overlooks Bangkok's most important shopping intersection. Take the elevator to the fourth floor to find it.

272 **GANESHA SHRINE**
AT: CENTRALWORLD
999/9 Rama I Road
Pathumwan ⓘ

Perhaps the most easily recognised shrine and deity, Ganesha is the pot-bellied elephant god who presides over artists seeking creativity. Also a Hindu god, but worshipped by Thais, you'll see constant devotees here in front of CentralWorld.

273 **TRIMURTI SHRINE**
IN FRONT OF: CENTRALWORLD
999/9 Rajadamri Road
Pathumwan ⓘ

Trimurti, located in front of CentralWorld, is a fusion of Shiva, Vishnu, and Brahma, and is a shrine for the lovelorn and those seeking romance. You'll see plenty of young women and men on their hands and knees here, with red roses, red incense sticks, and red candles, all praying for the flame of love to come their way.

274 MAE NAK SHRINE
AT: WAT MAHABUT
747 On Nut Soi 7/1
(Sukhumvit Soi 77)
Eastern Bangkok ⑫
+66 (0)94 098 7789

Belief in ghosts are a big part of Thai culture, and you'll see this in evidence at this shrine dedicated to the country's most famous ghost, Mae Nak, a woman whose husband went to the military, leaving her and her unborn infant alone to die. Women flock here to pray that conflict will not take their men away, with images of Mae Nak dominating the shrine.

275 ERAWAN SHRINE
Cnr. of Rajadamri Road
and Ploenchit Road
Pathumwan ①
+66 (0)2 254 1234

Built here 50 years ago to stop bad karma purportedly created when the neighbouring hotel foundations were laid on an inauspicious date, Erawan is Bangkok's most famous shrine. It is Hindu in origin, but worshipped by Thais and Chinese, and features live traditional dancers throughout the day.

5 spots to see
OLD BANGKOK

276 **KUDI JIN**
Thonburi ⑤

The square and maze of passageways built over waterways next to the Chao Phraya River is home to Bangkok's Portuguese community, dating from 1760. Wooden teak houses have Mary door knockers and Jesus portraits, and you'll find a longstanding bakery making three-generational traditional Portuguese snacks.

277 **YAOWARAT**
Chinatown ④

Yaowarat is Chinatown's main artery, filled with colourful shrines, Chinese signs, bird's nest soup restaurants, and delicious street food vendors. Come by day to explore the dilapidated narrow alleys, which lead off from Yaowarat, and by night to experience the old-world atmosphere and superb foodie scene.

278 **NANG LOENG**
Rattanakosin Island ③

This market area dates from the 1800s. The collection of tiny alleys was home to diverse immigrant groups, and became a vibrant community market, which today holds one of Bangkok's best food courts. You'll also find Thailand's oldest movie theatre here.

279 RATTANAKOSIN ISLAND
Rattanakosin Island ③

Originally an island surrounded by the river and a series of moats, Rattanakosin is one of the last places left in Bangkok without condominium, mall, or high-rise development, and remains the best place to navigate on foot. The country's most venerated spot, The Grand Palace, is here, as well as the iconic Giant Swing.

280 PHRAENG PHUTON
Rattanakosin Island ③

This charming square, reminiscent of an Italian piazza, remains off the tourist route. The square is surrounded by European neoclassical row houses, built by King Rama V in the early 1900s. Several restaurants are found here, serving single dish specialties that have been passed down for generations.

280 PHRAENG PHUTON

The 5 best
PARKS
to go to

---

281 BENJAKITTI PARK
Ratchadapisek Road
(Asoke)
Sukhumvit ⑦
+66 (0)2 254 1263

You'll forget about chaotic Bangkok at this lovely city centre oasis, crowded at sunset with locals walking, jogging, and riding bicycles. A paved bicycle path is separated from the pedestrian path, and goes 2 kilometres around the oval lake. You can rent both bicycles and rowboats/paddleboats for the lake.

282 LUMPHINI PARK
139/4 Witthayu
(Wireless) Road
Silom/Bang Rak ②
+66 (0)90 248 9874

This is Bangkok's largest central green area. Like Benjakitti, it features running, cycling, and boating, although over a more convoluted area. An added plus here: all the great areas for picnicking, and, during the cool season, free concerts on Sunday afternoons by the Bangkok Symphony.

283 KING RAMA IX PARK
Dok Mai, Prawet
Eastern Bangkok ⑫
+66 (0)92 438 2849

This large park in northeastern Bangkok is devoid of tourists and features a lotus lake with an exquisite Thai teak pavilion set in the middle of it. There are also lovely gardens here modelled on various countries around the world, abundant picnic space, and even a sports centre with a pool.

284 SUAN ROT FAI

Kamphaeng Phet 3
Road, Chatuchak
Northern Bangkok ⑪
+66 (0)2 537 9221

Suan Rot Fai means 'train park', a moniker given due to the fact that the Thailand State Railway owns the land here, but the park is anything but industrial, home to 150 acres of greenery, with bicycle loop trails and bike rental, plus a swimming pool, a kids' play area, and a really fantastic enclosed tropical butterfly garden.

285 SRI NAKHON KUENKHAN

Bang Krachao, Phra
Pradaeng
Southern Bangkok ⑬
+66 (0)91 174 7656

This is the centrepiece of Bang Krachao, Bangkok's 'lung' or open green space just across the Chao Phraya River, filled with shaded pavilions, picnic spaces, a large lake with kayaks and paddle boats for rent, and tranquil bike paths. The area feels miles away from urban Bangkok despite being just a two-minute boat ride across the river.

282 LUMPHINI PARK

5 great
OFF-THE-BEATEN-PATH
ATTRACTIONS

---

286 BANG KRACHAO

Phra Pradaeng
Southern Bangkok ⑬

Also known as Bangkok's 'lung', due to its shape from above, this is the largest open green space around Bangkok, only minutes from downtown across the Chao Phraya River. It's a wonderful oasis of elevated walkways above the water, where you can rent a bicycle and explore the 'floating' community.

287 SALA CHALERM THANI

35 Nakhon Sawan Road
Rattanakosin Island ③

Set in the old Nang Loeng market area, this was Thailand's first movie theatre, built in 1918 and made entirely of wood. Brass bands would accompany the early silent films and hundreds of people would attend during the theatre's heyday in the 1950s. Today the building still stands, hopefully awaiting preservation as a film museum.

288 KOH KRET ISLAND

287 SALA CHALERM THANI

289 TALING CHAN

288 KOH KRET ISLAND

Nonthaburi
Northern Bangkok ⑪

Koh Kret is an island in the north of Bangkok, both car-free and small enough to walk and cycle around. It is noted for its Mon temples and traditional pottery, and there is even a micro-brewery here to chill out at and watch the river go by.

289 TALING CHAN

Soi Chak Phra 17,
Taling Chan
Thonburi ⑤

Far more local and realistic than touristy Damnoen Saduak, this is a great option to take part in a Thai floating market. The market takes place on weekends and features canal-side boats that sell freshly grilled seafood. You can also go on boat tours to check out traditional canal life.

290 PAK KLONG TALAD BY NIGHT

Chak Phet Road
Rattanakosin Island ③

Bangkok's flower market is subdued by day, as not much is going on then, but it becomes a hive of working class activity at 2 to 3 in the morning, when massive deliveries of flowers are made by both boat and truck, all very colourful and atmospheric.

5

HISTORIC ATTRACTIONS

291 SANTA CRUZ CHURCH

112 Sai 1 Road
Thonburi ⑤
+66 (0)2 472 0153

This church, dating from 1769, is the centrepiece of the old Thai Catholic Sino-Portuguese community. It stands in a square reminiscent of Lisbon and is also known as the Chinese Church, due to the Chinese residents who helped assist in its upkeep. You'll even find a traditional five-generation Portuguese bakery down the atmospheric lanes leading from the church.

292 PHRA SUMEN FORT

148 Phra Athit Road
Banglamphu ⑨

The gleaming white brick and stucco fort standing along the river was built in 1783 to serve as a watchtower, and today is the only remnant of the old city wall that is in good condition. The fort was named after the mythical Mount Meru, a central peak in Buddhist-Hindu cosmology.

293 CHAO PHRAYA RIVER

Bangkok used to be known as the Venice of the East. While auto traffic rules the roost these days, travelling along the river by boat, next to many of the old historic colonial buildings and palaces, will let you see the city a bit more as it used to be.

291 **SANTA CRUZ CHURCH**

294 THE GRAND PALACE

Na Phra Lan Road
Rattanakosin Island ③
+66 (0)2 623 5500
www.palaces.thai.net

This is Bangkok's number one attraction, as well as the most venerated spot in the kingdom for Thais, so no matter how tired of temples you are, don't miss it. The revered Temple of the Emerald Buddha is the centrepiece here, but all of The Grand Palace complex is visually mind-boggling, with glittering golden chedis and stupas, along with immaculately crafted statues of various deities leading the sights. Do note that there is a dress code: shoulders and legs should be covered.

295 THE GOLDEN MOUNT
AKA: WAT SAKET

344 Chedi Phatipong
Rattanakosin Island ③
+66 (0)2 621 2280
www.watsraket.com

In the 1940s, the temple here was the tallest structure in Bangkok, used as a lookout for fire prevention! Prior to that, it had a grisly history of serving as the dumping ground for victims of the cholera plague in the 1880s. These days, you can climb to the golden chedi on top.

294 THE GRAND PALACE

5 great
NEIGHBOURHOODS
to check out

---

296 **THONGLOR**
ⓐ

Thonglor is one of Bangkok's trendiest neighbourhoods. Home to the majority of the Japanese expat population, it is packed with sushi and ramen restaurants, bars, and lots of clubs for the pretty and rich to party at.

297 **CHINATOWN**
④

Chinatown evokes the Bangkok of the past, full of narrow lanes. It's the best place in Bangkok to go for a walk, as well as to get lost in, and some of the sidestreets are now being spruced up with art projects and bohemian cafes. It really becomes atmospheric along Yaowarat Road by night, full of neon lights and food stalls.

298 **BANG RAK**
②

Bang Rak encompasses the riverside as well as Silom Road. You'll find the most atmospheric hotels along the river here, and on Charoen Krung Road some of the city's best street food vendors. Silom Road is home to the Patpong Night Bazaar and red light district, and it's all accessible by river ferry and Skytrain.

299 **SATHORN**

Also known as the Central Business District, Sathorn has Bangkok's greatest collection of skyscrapers. Mostly a working area by day, at night it becomes a hip hangout, with some great bars and international restaurants hidden on the sidestreets. Some of the best hotels are located here.

300 **THONBURI**

Thonburi encompasses all on the 'other' side of the Chao Phraya River. Much of it is built on canals, and hiring a longtail boat is the best way to go here. You'll find entire communities perched over the water here, and some of Bangkok's oldest and least visited sites.

5 lovely
BICYCLE TOURS

---

301 CO VAN KESSEL

River City, 23 Charoen
Krung Soi 24
Chinatown ②
+66 (0)2 639 7351
www.covankessel.com

This outfitter, started by a Dutchman over 30 years ago, focuses on tours around Chinatown and canals, combining the use of boats, bicycles, and walking to explore Bangkok's hidden alleyways and backroads. Their top tour lasts five hours, and they have a few shorter and longer options plus a few out of town trips.

302 BANGKOK VANGUARDS

4/4 Soi Troksin,
Tanao Road
Rattanakosin Island ③
+66 (0)85 833 9218
www.bangkok
vanguards.com

This newer outfitter gets rave reviews as it focuses on local interaction and on seeing Bangkok with more depth. They run an array of tours, two of which involve bicycles: one goes by night, discovering the bowels of Chinatown, while the other is a day trip out along canals, using van transport to return.

303 FOLLOW ME BIKE TOURS

126 (33/6) Sathorn Soi 9
Sathorn ⑥
+66 (0)87 059 1130
www.followme
biketour.com

A locally owned family business, Follow Me runs a wide array of trips at very reasonable prices. They wander around Chinatown, over to the canals of Thonburi, and through all of the city's old historic districts. Additionally, they have a fish foot spa set in their clubhouse for relaxing after a tour.

304 SPICE ROADS

45 (Sub Soi Pannee),
Soi Pridi Banomyong 26,
Sukhumvit Soi 71
Eastern Bangkok ⑫
+66 (0)2 381 7490
www.spiceroads.com

Spice Roads is a well run bike touring company that actually has trips all around the world. Their Bangkok branch runs sunset, Chinatown, and Bang Krachao jungle trips, as well as heading out of the city to some of the canals and up to the ancient city of Ayutthaya. They provide high-end mountain bikes along with trained guides.

305 GRASSHOPPER ADVENTURES

57 Ratchadamnoen
Klang Road
Rattanakosin Island ③
+66 (0)2 280 0832
www.grasshopper
adventures.com

Operating for over a decade, Grasshopper runs trips all across Asia. They are professional, safe, and well organised. They do bike tours to historic sites, along canals, by night, and also excellent food and cycling combos. They also do longer rides throughout Thailand.

304 SPICE ROADS

5
WALKS
to explore Bangkok

---

306 LITTLE ARABIA, AFRICA, AND RED LIGHT DISTRICT

Sukhumvit ⑦

Best done at night. Get off at the Nana BTS station and wander through Sukhumvit Soi 3/1, home to Bangkok's Little Arabia, full of spice traders, Middle Eastern restaurants, and shisha pipe teahouses. Just off of Soi 3, there is an alley with African bars and Ethiopian restaurants, a stark contrast to nearby Nana Plaza and Soi Cowboy.

307 RIVERSIDE RAMBLE

Silom/Bang Rak ②

From the Saphan Taksin BTS station, if you wander through the alleys heading north on the river, you will pass by the Assumption Cathedral, The East Asiatic Company, and the Old Customs House, all colonial landmarks of Bangkok's Venice of the East years.

308 LITTLE INDIA

Rattanakosin Island ③

Along Chakraphet Road, this area is known as Phahurat, and is home to Bangkok's Indian community. You'll find cheap dal and curry houses, textile shops, and a Sikh temple. The area adjoins Chinatown, so you can start your walk there, finishing with a river ferry home.

309 BACK ALLEYS OF CHINATOWN

Chinatown ④

Take the river ferry to the Harbour Department stop and wander into Chinatown via Soi Wanit 1. You'll come across narrow alleys, old shrines, streets full of rusted auto part shops, and packed neighbourhoods with a grimy working feel. This is the last bastion of the Bangkok of old.

310 SAOCHINGCHA

Rattanakosin Island ③

Starting from the photogenic iconic Giant Swing, this neighbourhood is home to a street of shops that sell golden Buddha images, plus lots of small one-dish restaurants that have been operating for almost 100 years. Make sure to check out Phraeng Phuton square, with its neoclassical architecture.

307 RIVERSIDE RAMBLE - THE EAST ASIATIC COMPANY

5
BIZARRE SIGHTS

311 WAT HUA KRABEU

Soi Thien Tha 19, Baan Khun Thian
Southern Bangkok ⑬
+66 (0)2 415 0532
www.wathuakrabeu.com

The eccentric abbot here, who formerly started an automotive garage for old Mercedes on the premises, has since turned his temple into a memorial for the water buffalo, which is in danger of extinction. The abbot gathers buffalo skulls here, which he intends to use to build a giant shrine and museum. It's one of Bangkok's oddest temples.

312 CHAO MAE TUBTIM

2 Wireless (Witthayu) Road (behind former Nai Lert Park Hotel)
Pathumwan ①

Women come here to pray prior to becoming pregnant. The shrine is also known as the phallus or penis shrine. It is set in a garden, and features hundreds of wooden phalluses of all sizes and shapes placed in offering, as the goddess of the shrine is a fertility spirit.

313 DAVID BECKHAM STATUE
AT: WAT PARIWAS

2/67 Rama III Soi 30 (Soi Pariwas)
Southern Bangkok ⑬
+66 (0)2 294 7711

During the 1998 World Cup, a Thai sculptor paid homage to the Thai mania for football, creating a gold statue of David Beckham, which was installed at the Wat Pariwas Temple. The temple's abbot was fine with this, saying: "Football is like a religion and has millions of followers!"

314 **THE GHOST TOWER**
AT: SATHORN UNIQUE TOWER
Charoen Krung Soi 53
Sathorn ⑥

This weird building started off as a luxury condominium but went bankrupt during the Southeast Asian financial crisis and was never finished. Locals claim that it is haunted, after years of squatters and derelicts, followed by thrill seekers who would bribe guards to climb and make videos.

315 **FORENSIC MUSEUM**
AT: SIRIRAJ HOSPITAL
2 Wanglang Road
Thonburi ⑤③
+66 (0)2 419 2619
www.sirirajmuseum.com

It's macabre, informative, and most certainly one of Bangkok's most unique attractions. The Forensic and Pathology museum here is a learning lab for forensic students at Siriraj University Hospital, and features mummified corpses of murderers and accident victims along with body parts, skeletons, and genetically mutated babies that sit floating in jars of formaldehyde.

312 CHAO MAE TUBTIM

311 WAT HUA KRABEU

STREET ART - CHAROEN KRUNG SOI 28

40 PLACES
TO ENJOY CULTURE

The 5 best
CINEMAS

316 **SCALA**
Siam Square Soi 2,
Rama I Road
Pathumwan ①
+66 (0)2 251 2861
www.apexsiam-square.com

Bangkok's elegant classical ode to the past, Scala opened in 1969, and today still hangs all the tiles of what's playing on the marquee by hand, with ushers wearing yellow blazers and bow ties. The lobby features an exquisite art deco design and winding staircase, and they still have classics revivals here.

317 **LIDO**
256 Rama I Road
Pathumwan ①
+66 (0)2 251 1265
www.apexsiam-square.com

While movie ticket prices across Bangkok seem to rise by the month, Lido keeps things the way they were, with 100 to 140-baht seats. The three theatres here show the best selection of art house, foreign, Oscar winners, and other films that depart from the Hollywood blockbuster norm.

318 **BANGKOK SCREENING ROOM**
1/3-7 Sala Daeng Soi 1
Silom/Bang Rak ②
+66 (0)90 906 3888
www.bkksr.com

This alternative screening room with 50 seats, a 4K projector, and digital surround sound supports independent films and screens a rotating list of classics, documentaries, and films that showcase emerging local filmmakers and talent. There is truffle popcorn and craft beer in the lobby to help you enjoy the shows.

319 **EMBASSY DIPLOMAT**
AT: CENTRAL EMBASSY,
6TH FLOOR
1031 Ploenchit Road
Pathumwan ⓘ
+66 (0)2 160 5999
www.embassycineplex.com

Reclining bed seats with pillows and blankets, an individual fridge stocked with beer and soft drinks, and personal service make this more like a luxury hotel stay than a movie outing, but that part is good too, with five private screening rooms and super comfortable cocoon chairs or the afore mentioned beds.

320 **ENIGMA**
AT: SIAM PARAGON, 6TH FLOOR
991 Rama I Road
Pathumwan ⓘ
+66 (0)2 129 4635
www.majorcineplex.com/
cinema/paragon-cineplex

There are only 34 sofas inside Enigma, where you and your partner can recline as if in bed. Bangkok's most expensive movie experience starts off with champagne, before moving on to appetisers, and you also get a 15-minute foot massage. You come here for the experience, regardless of what movie is being screened.

316 **SCALA**

5 of the most interesting
MUSEUMS

321 **NATIONAL MUSEUM**
4 Na Phra That Road
Rattanakosin Island ③
+66 (0)2 224 1333

Founded by King Rama V in 1887, Southeast Asia's largest museum is housed in a former palace and is full of artefacts that show off the full spectrum of Thai history, from the Ayutthaya and Sukhothai periods to the modern age. You'll find Thailand's biggest collection of art and artefacts here, all arranged by subject, ranging from armaments and clothing to palanquins and other pieces central to Thai history and culture.

322 **MUANG BORAN**
296/1 Sukhumvit Road,
Samut Prakan
Southern Bangkok
+66 (0)2 709 1644
www.ancientcitygroup.
net/ancientsiam

Muang Boran is an immense outdoor museum spread over 240 acres on grounds that are sculpted to resemble Thailand. There are over 100 miniature replicas of famous Thai temples or sites here, all of them placed on the grounds in geographic preciseness to their real counterparts. It's a great place to check out places like Ayutthaya and Sukhothai if you don't have the time to visit the real thing.

323 MUSEUM OF COUNTERFEIT GOODS

AT: TILLEKE & GIBBINS,
SUPALAI GRAND TOWER,
26TH FLOOR
1011 Rama III Road
Southern Bangkok ⑬
+66 (0)2 056 5546
www.tilleke.com/firm/
community/museum

This museum houses over 4000 items that infringe on trademarks, patents, and copyrights. Bangkok is infamous for its copied designer goods, pirated items, and more, and the museum tries to dispel the fact that counterfeiting is a victimless crime. As the display is set up in a law firm, you must contact them in advance to schedule a visit.

324 ERAWAN MUSEUM

99/9 Moo 1,
Bangmuangmai,
Samut Prakan
Eastern Bangkok ⑫
+66 (0)2 308 0305
www.ancientcitygroup.net/
erawan

This over the top museum combines fine and decorative arts to show off Thai culture. A massive 44 metre and 150 ton three-headed copper elephant statue at the gate is a prelude to what's to come, and the interior boasts sculpture-filled gardens, giant stained glass windows, and a psychedelic style.

325 MUSEUM OF SIAM

4 Sanam Chai Road
Rattanakosin Island ③
+66 (0)2 225 2777
www.ndmi.or.th

Also known as the Discovery Museum. There are many digital exhibits here for interactive learning, making it a great family spot, with a sign at the entrance saying 'please touch everything'. The museum focuses on the question of what it means to be Thai, tracing the history and ethnography of the country.

5
FESTIVALS
with a fantastic vibe

———

326 SONGKRAN
Held throughout Thailand
www.songkranday.com

Thais celebrate their New Year in April, and do so by hosting the world's biggest water fight. While traditionally a religious holiday in which Buddha images had water poured on them symbolising the washing away of sin, these days it includes water pistols out in the street, with everyone being fair game. Given that it is at the hottest time of year, it's a welcome relief for most folks.

327 VEGETARIAN FESTIVAL
Best to see in Phuket or in Bangkok Chinatown

This festival celebrates the Chinese emperor gods, with much of the city going vegetarian for the week. Of more interest to tourists will be the practices of devotees putting sharp objects through their cheeks and parading through the streets in one of the more macabre rites on the planet.

328 CHINESE NEW YEAR

329 ROP BUA

328 CHINESE NEW YEAR
Yaowarat Road
Chinatown ④

Bangkok's immense Thai-Chinese community ensures this is one of the biggest Chinese New Year celebrations in Asia. You can see traditional Chinese opera performed, watch dragon parades, and all of Chinatown turns into a massive street party full of great food and entertainment, with colourful shrines packed with worshippers as well.

329 ROP BUA LOTUS THROWING FESTIVAL
Wat Bang Phli Yai Nai, Moo 11, Bang Phli Yai, Samut Prakan Province Eastern Bangkok ⑫
+66 (0)32 471 502
www.watbang pleeyainai.org

This festival celebrates the end of the rainy season and pays homage to Buddha images that are carried by boat. What makes it special is that everyone throws lotus flowers at the images and into the canal, turning it into a giant flower throwing melee.

330 WAT BANG PHRA TATTOO FESTIVAL
Moo 3, Wat Lamut-Nara Phirom Road, Nakhon Chai Sri Nakhon Pathom Province (west of Bangkok)
+66 (0)34 389 333
www.bp.or.th

Every March this temple holds a bizarre ritual whereby devotees come to 'recharge' their mystical *'sak yant'* tattoos, purported to protect them from harm. They go into trances, and then proceed to act out their tattoos, which range from tigers to hermits to birds. The temple was made famous when Angelina Jolie got a tattoo here.

5 fascinating
ART GALLERIES

331 **KATHMANDU PHOTO GALLERY**
87 Pan Road
Silom/Bang Rak ②
+66 (0)2 234 6700
www.kathmandu photobkk.com

This cute little photo gallery is run by a prominent Thai photographer and is set in a restored pre-war shophouse in an Indian neighbourhood. There are prints of the owner on display, rotating exhibits, and a collection of Thai masters as well as up and coming local photographers. Art and spirituality books complete the collection.

332 **HOF ART**
288-290 Sukhumvit Road
Eastern Bangkok ⑫
+66 (0)2 178 0095
www.hofart-bkk.com

This contemporary art and exhibition space has put the normally drab eastern Bangkok onto the city cultural map. Set in the W District, which features a happening outdoor food court, Hof Art hosts rotating exhibits, provides art residencies, and sells paintings and sculptures by local artists.

333 **WTF GALLERY**
7 Sukhumvit Soi 51
Thonglor/Ekkamai ⑧
+66 (0)2 662 6246
www.wtfbangkok.com

This creative social club is part bar and part gallery, combining cool drinks with interesting art. The two upper floors showcase art exhibitions, and as it feels more like the home of a bunch of artist friends than a proper gallery, it is the least stuffy of all the Bangkok art venues.

334 BANGKOK ART & CULTURE CENTRE

939 Rama I Road
Pathumwan ①
+66 (0)2 214 6630
www.bacc.or.th

This large contemporary art centre redefined the Bangkok art scene, which was pretty much non existent at the time. The circular modern building, set around an atrium, has now been an iconic player for the Thai art community for over a decade, and hosts film, photography, and other art exhibitions.

335 SPEEDY GRANDMA GALLERY

672/52 Charoen Krung Road
Silom/Bang Rak ②
+66 (0)89 508 3859

This alternative art space supports Thai and international contemporary art and hosts talks and workshops that cater to a young bohemian crowd. The name is based on an urban legend of a grandmother who was cut in half in a motorbike accident, and the gallery seeks to spread the word about local art exactly as how local legends get passed around.

334 BANGKOK ART & CULTURE CENTRE

5 exciting
INDIE MUSIC
venues

---

336 STUDIO LAM
3/1 Sukhumvit Soi 51
Thonglor/Ekkamai ⑧
+66 (0)2 261 6661
www.zudrangma
records.com

Morlam is folk music from the northeast of Thailand, and it gets played with some funk at this alternative dive bar that is a contrast with the normal uber-trendy hipster bars that tend to dominate the Thonglor neighbourhood. Reggae and world beats are also in, but no mainstream or pop allowed here.

337 SOY SAUCE BAR
11/1 Charoen Krung
Soi 24
Chinatown ②
+66 (0)98 956 6549

From afro beats to jazz to dream pop, Soy Sauce hosts an array of indie performances along with exhibitions of avant-garde art and other alternative art and performance offerings. One of the new bars redefining the Chinatown hip scene, the space takes its name from its former life as a soy sauce making factory.

338 PLAY YARD
Lad Phrao Soi 8
Northern Bangkok ⑪
+66 (0)85 146 8017
www.playyard8.com

Every night brings different alternative live music at Play Yard, from hard rock to ska to funk and soul. It's a very local neighbourhood pub, so you'll see a lot of regulars here, mostly hanging out at the outdoor terrace.

339 JAM CAFE
**11 Soi Rong Nam Kang
(Charoen Rat Soi 1)
Sathorn ⑥
+66 (0)89 889 8059
*www.jambkk.com***

JAM has become Bangkok's top underground indie spot, serving as an all-encompassing space for artists and art lovers. There are short film festivals, underground movie nights, poetry readings, exhibitions, and usually at least three different indie music events each week.

340 FATTY'S BAR & DINER
**598/66 Din Daeng
Northern Bangkok ⑪
+66 (0)2 245 2965**

This dive bar has become a popular expat watering hole and the owner, a musician himself, brings in local indie bands on the weekends, as well as having some open mike nights during the week. Even when the music isn't playing, it's an unpretentious and inexpensive local bar with a great vibe.

340 FATTY'S BAR & DINER

5 *places to see*
TRADITIONAL THAI PERFORMANCE ARTS

341 **KHON DANCE**
66 Charoen Krung Road
Rattanakosin Island ③
+66 (0)2 222 0434
www.salachalerm krung.com

Sala Chalermkrung: Khon classical masked dance drama comes from the Thai royal court, and enacts scenes from the Indian Ramayana. One of the few places left to catch the elaborately costumed performances is at the historic Sala Chalermkrung, built in 1933 as Thailand's first air-conditioned cinema, and the first place where talking films were screened.

342 **SIAM NIRAMIT**
19 Tiamruammit Road, Huay Kwang
Northern Bangkok ⑪
+66 (0)2 649 9222
www.siamniramit.com

With over 100 performers and 500 costumes, this elaborate stage show traces Thai history and culture with three acts looking at Siam as a crossroads, Thai karma beliefs, and Buddhism as a unifying force. Besides the well choreographed stage production, there is also a perfectly replicated rural Thai village outside.

343 BAAN SILAPIN

315 Soi Wat Tong Sala
Ngam, Phet Kasem
Soi 28
Thonburi ⑤
+66 (0)2 868 5279

Hun lakhon lek, traditional Thai marionette puppetry, is hard to find these days, but at Baan Silapin, an old artist's house along one of the canals of Thonburi, you can still see it performed, with three masked performers manipulating the pulleys and levers bringing the puppets to life, performing tales from the Ramakien, Thailand's historic epic.

344 MUAY THAI LIVE

AT: ASIATIQUE THE
RIVERFRONT
2194 Charoen Krung
Road
Southern Bangkok ⑬
+66 (0)2 108 5999
www.muaythailive.com

Muay Thai boxing may be a bit excessive for some, as combatants use both arms and legs to land punches and blows with explosive force, but this stage presentation, featuring a choreographed live performance with professional boxers, softens the blows, and shows the history, traditions, and skill involved in this unique sport, which is integral to Thailand's cultural history.

345 CALYPSO CABARET

AT: ASIATIQUE
THE RIVERFRONT
2194 Charoen Krung
Road
Southern Bangkok ⑬
+66 (0)2 688 1415
www.calypsocabaret.com

Despite the sound of it, this is a very family friendly transvestite cabaret show, with the costumes and dance routines, mixing foreign hit songs and Thai music, being a knockout, and the girls, er, um, guys, superbly gifted, with a good number of them having performed internationally.

343 BAAN SILAPIN

344 MUAY THAI LIVE

345 CALYPSO CABARET

5 tours or classes to
EXPERIENCE THAI CULTURE

---

346 COOKING WITH POO
Khlong Toei Market
Southern Bangkok ⑬
+66 (0)87 686 3714
www.cookingwithpoo.com

Despite the rather unsanitary sounding name (Poo here actually refers to the host's nickname), this excellent cooking school was started by a food seller in the Khlong Toei slum of Bangkok. Poo will take you shopping in the local wet market, teach you authentic Thai recipes, and show you a side of the city you'd probably never see otherwise.

347 CHILI PASTE FOOD TOUR
Rattanakosin Island ③
+66 (0)94 552 2361
www.foodtours
bangkok.com

Energetic Chin, who is passionate about preserving authentic Thai cuisine, runs the city's best food tour. She takes you to off-the-beaten-path local markets to sample the best hard-to-find dishes, and gives a real insight into Thai street food culture. Group size is kept to 6 and tours include at least 15 dishes, so prepare to gorge!

348 APSARA RIVER CRUISE

AT: BANYAN TREE HOTEL
**21/100 South Sathorn
Road
Sathorn ⑥
+66 (0)2 679 1200**
*www.banyantree.com/
en/ap-thailand-bangkok/
apsara*

The Banyan Tree's Apsara tour sets itself apart from the ordinary tour boat scene by using a reconverted vintage rice barge decked out in traditional decor to sail on the Chao Phraya, and the small group size makes for a more enjoyable way to experience river life. The tour also includes a multi-course authentic Thai dinner, making it worth a splurge.

349 BLUE ELEPHANT COOKING SCHOOL

**233 South Sathorn
Road
Sathorn ⑥
+66 (0)2 673 9353**
*www.blueelephant
cookingschool.com*

Chef Nooror has presided over this Thai cuisine empire for over a decade, and the Blue Elephant Restaurant is considered one of Bangkok's top fine dining venues. They do an excellent 'ancient Thai cuisine' course that focuses on long forgotten dishes. The 1903 colonial Thai China Building the cooking class is housed in, is an added plus.

350 EXPIQUE: THE MARKET EXPERIENCE

**46 Sathorn Soi 9
Sathorn ⑥
+66 (0)85 873 3308**
*www.expique.com/
bangkok/the-market-
experience*
*www.market
experiences.com*

Expique focuses on unique and personalised Bangkok experiences, and their Market Experience tour takes visitors inside the Pak Khlong Talad Flower Market, spending several hours behind the scenes, visiting vendors, and seeing how the market really works.

5 places to appreciate
STREET ART

351 **CHAROEN KRUNG SOI 32**
Charoen Krung Soi 32
Bang Rak ②

The BUKRUK Urban Arts Festival in 2016 brought global artists to Bangkok in an attempt to enhance it as an Asian art capital. This alley by the river was one of the centrepieces for street murals, and all of them have remained intact. Noted Thai artist Alex Face has his iconic bunny character, Mardi, painted here.

352 **RATCHATHEWI-SAEN SAB CANAL**
Hua Chang Bridge Pier,
Phaya Thai Rd
Pathumwan ①

If you walk west on the pathway along the Saen Sab Canal from the Hua Chang pier, you'll find long murals painted on both sides of the canal, brightening up the waterside community. The wall paintings were some of the first collaborations between Thai and European street artists.

353 **TROK SAN CHAO RONG KUEAK**
Trok San Chao Rong
Kueak/Soi Wanit 1 Road
Chinatown ④

This winding alley deep in China-town seeks to emulate the Georgetown, Penang street art that has helped give the Malaysian city UNESCO status. There are lifelike wall paintings that blend in with the neighbourhood, like windows, pipes, and people sitting against the façades.

354 CHAROEN KRUNG SOI 28
Charoen Krung Soi 28
Bang Rak ②

Korean artist Daehyun Kim has a beautifully detailed black and white traditional East Oriental scene from his Moonassi series here. There are also two immense murals by Romanian illustrator and muralist Saddo and Thai artist Bon, who painted his iconic bird Pukruk riding a unicycle. Make sure to cross Charoen Krung for more murals in the opposite alleyway.

355 CHALERMLA PARK
Soi Si Surut/Petchaburi
Soi 18
Pathumwan ①

This small park hidden just south of the Ratchathwei Skytrain station is home to an excellent collection of graffiti street art. Alex Face and Bon, two of the top Thai street artists, feature prominently here. In the recent past, several excellent paintings – honouring the in 2016 deceased Thai King Bhumibol – have been done, adding to the vibe.

353 TROK SAN CHAO RONG KUEAK

QUEEN SAOVABHA SNAKE FARM

25 THINGS TO DO
WITH CHILDREN

The 5 best
ATTRACTIONS
for kids

---

356 QUEEN SAOVABHA SNAKE FARM

1871 Rama IV Road
Pathumwan ②
+66 (0)2 252 0161
www.saovabha.com

The Snake Farm is Bangkok's top educational and whole-family-fun tourist attraction. The 'farm' is part of the Queen Saovabha Memorial Institute and the Red Cross, where they do toxin and anti-venom research. In addition to a highly informative museum, there is live venom extraction every day, as well as the highlight snake show which the kids will adore.

357 DREAM WORLD

62 Moo 1, Rangsit-
Ongkarak Road, km 7,
Thanyaburi
Northern Bangkok ⑪
+66 (0)2 577 8666
www.dreamworld.co.th

This small scale amusement park has something for the whole family. There is a Skycoaster roller coaster, a white water rafting ride, bumper cars and boats, a -4° snow town with sleigh rides, a haunted mansion, and a 4D adventure movie that lets you get involved. Kids of all ages will find something of interest here.

358 FUNARIUM

111/1 Sukhumvit Soi 26
Sukhumvit ⑦
+66 (0)2 665 6555
www.funarium.co.th

For parents who want to chill out with a massage while their young ones play to their heart's content, this is it. Highlights include a giant padded playground, trampolines, a bike and skate track, an arts and crafts area, and even a Thai cooking class. Best of all: it's entirely supervised.

359 KIDZANIA

AT: SIAM PARAGON,
5TH FLOOR
991 Rama I Road
Pathumwan ①
+66 (0)2 683 1888
www.bangkok.
kidzania.com

Edu-tainment at its best, Kidzania is an entire replica city built for kids, complete with shops, where children get involved in all aspects. They open bank accounts with kidzo currency, they can work as a mechanic, fly a plane or be a reporter, and parents are only allowed to watch, leaving the kids in charge of all the decisions.

360 FLOW HOUSE

AT: A-SQUARE
120/1 Sukhumvit Soi 26
Sukhumvit ⑦
+66 (0)2 108 5210
www.flowhouse
bangkok.com

If you want to take the kids to the beach without leaving town, Flow House takes care of things. This in-city surf club has an imported simulated wave surfing machine that allows you to boogie board and surf just like in the ocean. Guided instruction and equipment is included in the admission price.

The 5 best
ICE-CREAM shops

361 NUTTAPORN

94 Phraeng Phuton
Square
Rattanakosin Island ③
+66 (0)2 222 2686

An old auntie and her two sisters run this third generation hole-in-the-wall ice-cream shop, which has been in business for more than 70 years. They do homemade fresh coconut, matcha, and mango ice cream made from the revered *maha chanuk* mangoes. The shop is located in the beautiful neoclassical Phraeng Phuton square.

362 ALL COCO

141 Thonglor Soi 10
Thonglor/Ekkamai ⑧
+66 (0)2 138 0628
www.allcoco.co.th

This company started out exporting coconuts, promoting Thai coconuts, and later made packaged coconut ice cream. Now they have a full dessert cafe where you can feast on fresh ice cream served as a sandwich (3 scoops in a hot dog bun!), on grilled waffles, or in smoothies.

363 FARM TO TABLE

179 Atsadang Road
Rattanakosin Island ③
+66 (0)2 115 2625

This old town hidden away cafe serves up organic ice cream and Italian-style gelato. Everything here is organic, from the vegetables used for Thai dishes to the milk used for the ice cream. Try the grass jelly and jackfruit gelato and kick back out of the heat, it's a great little spot.

364 BEN & JERRY'S
AT: SIAM PARAGON, G/F

991/1 Rama I Road
Pathumwan ①
+66 (0)2 610 7620
www.benjerry.co.th

From a refurbished gas station shop in Burlington, Vermont, to being the most recognised gourmet ice cream in the world, Ben & Jerry's opened a Bangkok shop in Siam Paragon in 2016 to lines around the mall. These days it's a bit calmer, and you can get their most popular favourites, like Chunky Monkey or Cherry Garcia, here.

365 EMACK & BOLIO'S
AT: EMQUARTIER, HELIX ZONE,
7TH FLOOR

637 Sukhumvit Road
Sukhumvit ⑦
+66 (0)2 294 0081
www.emackand
boliosthai.com

This gourmet ice cream was started by some hippies in the 1970s in Boston, making fresh homemade ice cream to satisfy the sweet tooth among touring rock stars. The snazzy EmQuartier shop serves up ice-cream pizzas, cakes, cones dipped in marshmallow-coated cereal, and smoothies and yogurt, all using premium grade ice cream made from natural cow's milk.

361 NUTTAPORN

5 fun
CHILDREN'S MUSEUMS

366 **BANGKOK DOLLS**
85 Soi Mo Leng,
off Ratchaprarop Soi 22
Northern Bangkok ⑪
+66 (0)2 245 3008
www.bangkokdolls.com

Tongkorn Chandavimol is an extraordinary dollmaker and founder of this unusual museum, made up of her collection of 500 handmade dolls, done up in traditional hill tribe garb or as traditional Thai puppets. The museum will help young kids understand Thailand's rich culture.

367 **CHILDREN'S DISCOVERY MUSEUM**
810 Kamphaeng Phet
Soi 4
Northern Bangkok ⑪
+66 (0)2 272 4500

A Thai kitchen, an art studio, and a dino-detective zone are just part of this hands-on kids' museum. Children get to dress up in costume and role play, become detectives to dig for dinosaur bones, and get wet in the fountain and rain-shower-filled Water Zone. It's good supervised fun.

368 **SCIENCE SQUARE**
AT: CHAMCHURI SQUARE,
5TH FLOOR
Cnr. of Rama IV Road
and Phayathai Road
Pathumwan ②
+66 (0)2 160 5356
www.nsm.or.th

This city branch of the National Science Museum (the main branch is in a northern suburb) is super child-friendly, with hands on exhibits and play areas. An excavation pit beckons amateur fossil finders, there's a science lab with ongoing experiments, and a dialogue in the dark, where blind guides lead you through darkened rooms.

369 NATIONAL MUSEUM OF ROYAL BARGES

80/1 Arun Amarin Road
Thonburi ⑤③
+66 (0)2 424 0004

Kids will enjoy the ornate gold-covered teak barges that are housed here. The barges were used regularly in Bangkok's Venice of the East days, but are now only taken out for the Royal Barge Procession ceremony each year. Half the fun is getting here, as it's in the Bangkok Noi canal, so taking a longtail boat here makes it really atmospheric.

370 ART IN PARADISE

AT: ESPLANADE MALL,
4TH FLOOR
99 Ratchadaphisek Road
Northern Bangkok ⑪
+66 (0)2 660 9130
www.artinparadise
bkk.co.th

This interactive 3D art gallery lets you get into the pictures. There are Van Gogh and Dutch Masters paintings to climb into, hanging bridges or cliff tops to stand on, and sharks and gorillas leaping right out of the frames. It's one of the most Instagram and Facebook friendly selfie hangouts you'll find in town.

370 ART IN PARADISE

5 wonderful shops for
KIDS' CLOTHING

---

371 DEEPER KIDS
AT: PLATINUM FASHION MALL,
2ND FLOOR, ZONE 2
222 Petchaburi Road
Pathumwan ①
+66 (0)86 036 6398

Deeper Kids started out making custom made jeans for children some 20 years ago. Formerly known as Deeper Jeans, they've now expanded to doing all types of kids' clothing, making shirts, pants, skirts, and even fashionable belts for families who want to outfit their little ones. They do just about anything for children aged 6 months to 18 years.

372 LOTTIE & MAX
AT: THE TERRACE
49 Sukhumvit Soi 49
Sukhumvit ⑦
+66 (0)2 662 5896
www.the49terrace.com/
lottie.html

If your 7-or-under-year old has an inner fashionista ready to come out, this is the place to bring him or her. Lottie & Max do contemporary designs with smart and vibrant attire, along with bed linens and beach-going items like towels, swimsuits, hats, and flip-flops.

373 HALLO HEIDI

AT: PLATINUM FASHION MALL,
5TH FLOOR, ZONE 1

222 Petchaburi Road
Pathumwan ①
+66 (0)87 695 3355

Hallo Heidi is another top kids' clothing shop in the family-friendly Platinum Fashion Mall: their entire 5th floor is filled with children's clothing shops. They do super cute and snazzy dresses, skirts, pants, and shirts for the little ones, and will have your kid looking like a Bangkok model in no time.

374 BABY PEAK

AT: PLATINUM FASHION MALL,
5TH FLOOR, ZONE 1

222 Petchaburi Road
Pathumwan ①
+66 (0)2 121 9840
www.babypeak.com

BaBy PeAk specialises in baby and children's shoes, as well as pyjamas, scarves, and plenty more. Their designs are stylish and warm, and range from cartoon-covered Crocs to rubber duck sandals and fashionable little boots. The prices here are dirt cheap too, with most items ranging from 200 to 500 baht.

375 NATURALLY BEBE

9/2-3 Tana Arcade Alley,
Sukhumvit Soi 63
Thonglor/Ekkamai ⑧
+66 (0)2 381 8300
www.naturallybebe.com

Naturally BeBe calls itself not only a baby clothing store, but a new parents' shop as well. They have an extensive range of items for newborns, from baby strollers and nursing bras to organic baby shoes and clothing, as well as learning toys, bath items, and much more. For infants, this is Bangkok's finest shop.

5

CHILD-FRIENDLY

restaurants

376 **CAFE TARTINE**
65 Wireless (Witthayu)
Road
Pathumwan ⑦
+66 (0)2 168 5464
www.cafetartine.net

This French bakery cafe has a full kid's menu (with kid-sized portions), as well as a whole collection of colouring books, crayons, and even kids' movies playing in the corner throughout the day, and plenty of families come here with their little ones, so there's always company.

377 **MR. JONES ORPHANAGE**
AT: SIAM CENTER, 3RD FLOOR
979 Rama I Road
Pathumwan ①
+66 (0)2 658 1163
*www.mrjones
international.com*

Bangkok design mogul Ashley Sutton made this unique cake shop and dessert restaurant which is full of stuffed teddy bears, toys, and actually the opposite of what a sterile Dickensian orphanage might be. Wooden trains run through the shop, seats are meant for little people, and the red velvet cheesecake, bubble waffles, and other sweets are simply ravishing.

378 CHARLEY BROWN'S

19/9-10 Sukhumvit Soi 19
Sukhumvit ⑦
+66 (0)2 044 2553

Adults will be busy with margaritas here, but the Mexican food is for the whole family. Charley Brown's provides a kids' menu with mini burritos, milkshakes, plus colouring books, crayons, and an activity page, not to mention highchairs for the tiny ones.

379 GASTRO 1/6

RMA Institute, Soi
Sai Namthip 2, 238
Sukhumvit Soi 22
Sukhumvit ⑦
+66 (0)80 603 6421

The poached egg or Iberian ham tortilla breakfasts here are as nice as the hidden garden bistro. Families will like the children's portions of various breakfast options, and the peanut butter and bananas on toast are aimed specifically at kids. Bring along a book and some games and you might settle in here all morning.

380 SLAPPY CAKES

1/10-11 Sukhumvit Soi 39
Sukhumvit ⑦
+66 (0)2 662 4887

Both kids and adults will be totally immersed at this U.S. chain import that features all day breakfast and lets you create your own pancakes. You get different flavoured pancake batter squeezers, plus toppings like banana, chocolate chips, nuts, mangoes, and more to create your own and then throw on the griddle at your table.

THE SIAM HOTEL

35 PLACES
TO SLEEP

The 5 most
E L E G A N T
stays

381 **MANDARIN ORIENTAL**
48 Oriental Avenue
Silom/Bang Rak ②
+66 (0)2 659 9000
www.mandarinoriental.
com/bangkok

The Grande Dame of all Bangkok stays, the Mandarin Oriental oozes colonial charm. Somerset Maugham, Graham Greene, and Joseph Conrad stayed here, and the setting overlooking the Chao Phraya River is as romantic as it gets. The classy restaurants, bars, and superlative service put it ahead of all the others.

382 **THE ST. REGIS**
159 Rajadamri Road
Pathumwan ①
+66 (0)2 207 7777
www.stregisbangkok.com

Private butlers and a view of the horse races at the Royal Sports Club across the way are just some of the perks at this swank downtown hotel, along with a century-old champagne sabering tradition at the bar each night, and other regal offerings.

383 **SIAM KEMPINSKI**
991/9 Rama I Road
Pathumwan ①
+66 (0)2 162 9000
www.kempinski.com/en/
bangkok/siam-hotel

Set behind Bangkok's most glitzy mall, Siam Paragon, the Siam Kempinski has crystal chandeliers and marble floors, yet the hotel feels more like an island escape, with rooms with direct pool access set around an enormous free-form set of swimming pools.

384 THE SIAM HOTEL

3/2 Khao Road
Dusit ⑩
+66 (0)2 206 6999
www.thesiamhotel.com

Set away from the crowds in historic Dusit, the Siam is Bangkok's most expensive stay. Catering to the 5-star traveller who wants privacy and exclusivity, its hidden Old City Chao Phraya location makes it the perfect choice for those seeking solitude. It is impeccably run by a well-heeled family of noted Thai musicians and actors.

385 SHANGRI-LA

89 Soi Wat Suan Plu
Silom/Bang Rak ②
+66 (0)2 236 7777
www.shangri-la.com/
bangkok

Long considered one of Asia's best stays, the Shangri-La takes you back to the city's 'Venice of the East' days, with tranquil gardens and dazzling views right at the city heart of the Chao Phraya River. Its spa has won awards worldwide, and the swimming pool is one of Bangkok's largest.

384 THE SIAM HOTEL

The 5 best
SMALL
hotels

---

386 CHAKRABONGSE VILLAS

396 Maharat Road
Rattanakosin Island ③
+66 (0)2 222 1290
www.thaivillas.com

Once the residence of a Thai prince, whose daughter refurbished it as a gorgeous upscale and intimate lodging. Three traditional Thai teak villas were transported down the river to the location here in 1908, and they are the epitome of elegance and privacy. There are only 4 suites/rooms here, so book well ahead.

387 ARIYASOM VILLA

65 Sukhumvit Soi 1
Sukhumvit ⑦
+66 (0)2 254 8880
www.ariyasom.com

The original owner of this 1942 villa was a Thai engineer who designed the National Stadium and built water pipes across the Chao Phraya River. His granddaughter and her foreign husband have renovated the lovely property.

388 BAAN CHANTRA

120/1 Samsen Road
Banglamphu ⑨
+66 (0)2 628 6988
www.baanchantra.com

This 1930s traditional Thai teak house has only four rooms, and it's a good choice for those wanting the Khao San Road backpacker vibe with a bit more style. The rooms are cosy and some have small patios. Located near the river, it's atmospheric and an escape from the nearby Khao San craze.

389 THE CABOCHON
14/29 Sukhumvit Soi 45
Sukhumvit ⑦
+66 (0)2 259 2871
www.cabochonhotel.com

Only four villas and suites make up the intimate Cabochon Hotel, a colonial hotel that brings back the nostalgia and charms of the roaring and chic 1920s in Shanghai. Rooms feature antique lamps, vintage armchairs and writing desks, wood-framed vanity mirrors, French double doors and fine Belgian linens.

390 SALA RATTANAKOSIN
39 Maharat Road
Rattanakosin Island ③
+66 (0)2 622 1388
www.salarattanakosin.com

This four-storey boutique hotel has just 15 rooms, with about half of them boasting some of the best views of Wat Arun from the giant bedroom windows, with sweeping views of the Chao Phraya right at your feet. The River View Suite even has a large circular bathtub from which to gape at the scenery.

390 SALA RATTANAKOSIN

5 tasteful
DESIGN
hotels

---

391 **SOFITEL SO**

2 North Sathorn Road
Sathorn ⑥ ②
+66 (0)2 624 0000
www.so-sofitel-
bangkok.com

A group of elite Thai architects and French haute couturier mogul Christian Lacroix designed this cutting edge property, with rooms and spaces designed around the five elements theme. Rooms have open plan bathtubs and come with free Mac Mini's, and everything overlooks Lumphini Park and the glittering Bangkok skyline.

392 **SIAM@SIAM BY DESIGN**

865 Rama I Road
Pathumwan ①
+66 (0)2 217 3000
www.siamatsiam.com

A hip urban hotel for the young at heart, with one of Bangkok's most innovative interiors, it's a vibrant place to hang out. Rooms come in Biz Class and Leisure Class and have large picture windows and loud exciting colours, and there is traditionalist modern art everywhere you look.

393 **THE W**

106 North Sathorn Road
Sathorn ⑥
+66 (0)2 344 4000
www.whotelbangkok.com

The cutting-edge W excels in urban hip. Rooms come with names like Wonderful, Spectacular, and Fantastic instead of Standard, Deluxe, and Premier, and are furnished with electronic pads for room controls, 40" flat-screen televisions, and even pet beds upon request. It's a young, fun, and very chic place.

394 HOTEL INDIGO

81 Witthayu (Wireless)
Road
Pathumwan ⓘ
+66 (0)2 207 4999
www.ihg.com/hotelindigo

Colourful rooms, gold sinks, hardwood floors, black and white wall photos, and plenty of eclectic vibe make Bangkok's first Indigo property a winner. Set over Lumphini Park, the 5-star hotel features walls of wireless radios showing off the history of Wireless Road, and there is an infinity-edge pool on the roof.

395 MYSTIC PLACE

224/5-9 Pradipat Road,
Phayathai
Northern Bangkok ⓘ
+66 (0)2 270 3344
www.mysticplacebkk.com

This small boutique hotel has 36 individually themed rooms, all with plenty of loud colour, recycled art pieces, funky cartoons, movie posters, and other bric-à-brac. In fact, the hotel resembles an avant-garde art gallery far more than a lodging. It's convenient for Chatuchak Market, and there is a free shuttle to the Skytrain.

391 SOFITEL SO

The 5 best
HOSTELS

396 LUB D SIAM

925/9 Rama I Road
Pathumwan ①
+66 (0)2 612 4999
www.lubd.com/
siamsquare

Lub D has turned hosteling into boutique hipness, with sparkling clean, colourful rooms that feature stencil art, along with accommodating staff who organise pub crawls and more. Travellers can choose from tidy 4-person dorms and also twin and double rooms, all of which have free Wi-Fi and electronic keycard access.

397 NIRAS BANKOC

204-206 Mahachai Road
Rattanakosin Island ③
+66 (0)2 221 4442
www.nirasbankoc.com

This old town property is set in a traditional shophouse featuring Sino-Portuguese architecture that dates from the late 1800s, and was actually owned by a prince. It has only seven rooms, with a choice of dorms or private digs, and the old teak home feels far more like a museum than a place to stay.

398 BED STATION

486/149-150 Soi
Petchaburi 16,
Petchaburi Road
Pathumwan ①
+66 (0)2 019 5477
www.bedstationhostel.com

This hip urban hostel looks like a Greenwich Village coffee shop. The interior has a modern industrial minimalist design featuring a red brick foyer. Dorm beds have their own private curtains and lights, bathrooms have rainfall shower heads, and there is even a relax room with beanbag cushions and games.

399 NAPPARK

5 Tani, Khwaeng Talad
Yot
Banglamphu ⑨
+66 (0)2 282 2324
www.nappark.com

NapPark has all the modern features a young hostel visitor could want. Dorm beds each have a plug, locker, and curtains for privacy, there is a chilled out common room with beds to kick back on and movies screened throughout the day, and it is on a quiet side street near Khao San Road.

400 THE YARD

51 Phahonyothin Road,
Samsen Nai
Northern Bangkok ⑪
+66 (0)89 677 4050
www.theyardhostel.com

This unique hostel is made from converted shipping containers and also has a private garden with hammocks, plus dorms with private reading lights. They also hold parties open to all in the yard, with themes like face painting or yoga, making it a very communal place with a friendly vibe.

The 5 best
ROOMS WITH A VIEW

---

401 THE TOWER CLUB AT LEBUA
1055 Silom Road
Silom/Bang Rak ②
+66 (0)2 624 9555
www.lebua.com/tower-club

Suites here start from the 51st floor and up, and all come with massive balconies which overlook the Chao Phraya River and neon cityscape. The hotel is high enough to make neighbouring hotels and condominiums appear like shacks. Those who want to splurge can rent the Hangover Suite, used by the Hollywood film cast.

402 INN A DAY
57-61 Maharat Road
Rattanakosin Island ③
+66 (0)2 221 0577
www.innaday.com

This family-run hotel is built in an old warehouse. Its upper level suite rooms look straight out at the iconic Wat Arun, one of Bangkok's most photographed monuments. You can awaken to the golden sunrise illuminating the top of the temple, and else enjoy sunsets over the river.

403 THE CHATRIUM RIVERSIDE

28 Charoen Krung Road
Sathorn ⑥
+66 (0)2 307 8888
www.chatrium.com

The Chatrium boasts several tall tower buildings which give elevated views straight down the Chao Phraya River, plus a bird's eye view of the giant ferris wheel at the Asiatique night market. South of the main riverside hotels, it's a hidden charmer.

404 THE BANYAN TREE

21/100 South Sathorn Road
Sathorn ⑥
+66 (0)2 679 1200
www.banyantree.com

While it is hard to top the 360 degrees panoramas from the rooftop Moon Bar, the rooms some ten floors below in the same property are almost as good. The upper floor suites and Club rooms have dizzying river and city views, with all of Bangkok's best skyscrapers right in front of you.

405 THE PENINSULA

333 Charoennakorn Road
Thonburi ⑤
+66 (0)2 020 2888
www.bangkok.
peninsula.com

There are plenty of luxury hotels in Bangkok, but most of them sit on the Bangkok side of the Chao Phraya River. The Peninsula gives the added bonus of looking not only at the river view, but at the dazzling array of skyscrapers behind it, as well as at all the old colonial buildings along the waterfront.

The 5 most
U N U S U A L
places to sleep

---

406 PHRANAKORN-NORNLEN

46 Thewet Soi 1
Dusit ⑩
+66 (0)2 628 8188
www.phranakorn-
nornlen.com

Super funky boutique guesthouse with rooms turned by the artist owner into colourful, almost psychedelic experiences, with large vibrant wall murals. Her paintings also adorn all the hallways, and the large open space downstairs has recreated a traditional Thai community, and oozes plenty of charm.

407 SOOK STATION

45-49 Sukhumvit Soi
101/2
Eastern Bangkok ⑫
+66 (0)86 332 0555
www.sookstation.com

At this novel hostel, you're given convict pyjamas, and your inmate number serves in place of a key. Your room also has iron bars, as this Shawshank Redemption-inspired place really does resemble a prison. Don't sweat it too much though, there is a hot tub on the roof should you need to escape.

408 SHANGHAI MANSION

479-481 Yaowarat Road
Chinatown ④
+66 (0)2 221 2121
www.shanghai
mansion.com

Located right in the heart of Chinatown, Shanghai Mansion looks like something right out of 1930s Shanghai. The design is Chinese Art Deco, and rooms are filled with warm colours, old photographs, and giant claw tubs. There's also a vintage jazz bar upstairs, accessed via an iron spiral staircase.

409 PRAYA PALAZZO

757/1 Somdej
Prapinklao Soi 2
Thonburi ⑤⑨
+66 (0)2 883 2998
www.prayapalazzo.com

This unique hotel is a former Italian mansion that has become a hidden boutique property. You can only get here by boat, although the hotel does have its own private ferry for guests and gives everyone a cell phone to use. Rooms feature Italian antiques and wooden floors, and there are only 17 rooms. Kids under 12 are not allowed.

410 BANGKOK TREEHOUSE

60 Moo 1, Petch Cha
Hueng Road, Phra
Pradaeng, Samut
Prakarn
Southern Bangkok ⑬
+66 (0)82 995 1150
www.bangkok
treehouse.com

Bangkok Treehouse is one of a kind. The eco-friendly boutique hotel sits on a bicycle path in Bang Krachao, the green 'lungs' of the city, located across the Chao Phraya River. You can come here by boat or cycle in. Try the 'View With a Room' which features a bed with mosquito netting out on an open bamboo deck.

406 PHRANAKORN-NORNLEN

5

AFFORDABLE

places to sleep

---

411 **IBIS RIVERSIDE**

27 Soi Charoen Nakhon
17, Klongsan
Thonburi ⑤
+66 (0)2 659 2888
www.ibis.com

You will normally pay a fortune to stay on the river in Bangkok, but the Ibis is a wonderful exception, with small rooms under 2000 baht set on the tranquil Thonburi side, looking across at all the Bangkok landmarks. There's a riverside swimming pool plus a free shuttle to get across the river.

412 **DREAM**

10 Sukhumvit Soi 15
Sukhumvit ⑦
+66 (0)2 254 8500
www.dreamhotels.com/
bangkok

This contemporary hotel attracts visitors with mood-lit rooms and glowing lights. Normally, you'll pay a premium for fancy places like this that are in the heart of Sukhumvit, but here you'll get easy access to the Terminal 21 Mall, the Skytrain and metro, and hundreds of restaurants and bars, without having to break the bank.

413 BANGKOK CITY HOTEL

268 Soi Petchaburi 10-
12, Petchaburi Road
Pathumwan ①
+66 (0)2 215 2929
www.bangkokcityhotel.com

Rooms are pretty ordinary here, but consistently come in at under 1500 baht, even in high season. You get a mini-bar, satellite TV, free Wi-Fi, an inclusive buffet breakfast, and there is even an indoor swimming pool upstairs. There's a free shuttle to Pratunam for shopping, plus a great local food scene down the street.

414 BANGKOK LOFT INN

55 Somdet Phra Chao
Taksin Road
Thonburi ⑤
+66 (0)2 862 0300
www.bangkokloftinn.com

This small hotel is located on the Thonburi side of the river, well away from the tourist trade, but its location next to a Skytrain station means you can be in the city centre within 15 minutes. Rooms here go for around 1200 baht and have flat-screen televisions and coffee-makers, plus breakfast is included.

415 BAAN DINSO

78/3 Ratchadamnoen
Road
Rattanakosin Island ③
+66 (0)96 556 9795
www.baandinso.com/
Ratchadamnoen

This boutique budget-hotel has an excellent location by Democracy Monument, making it easy to explore Old Bangkok and Khao San Road. Rooms are small but spotless, there's a garden, a snazzy cafe, and just about every room goes for less than 2000 baht, with those with outside bathrooms dropping all the way down to 650.

KEMPINSKI THE SPA

30 PLACES
TO GET PAMPERED

---

5 *exhilarating*
SPA SPLURGES

---

416 THE ORIENTAL SPA
AT: MANDARIN ORIENTAL

48 Oriental Avenue
Silom/Bang Rak ②
+66 (0)2 659 9000
www.mandarinoriental.
com/bangkok/luxury-spa

Here you can try a unique 'muay thai' spa in which the deep oil massage uses knees and elbows to simulate the kicks and punches of Thai boxing. From herbal wraps to Swedish to traditional Thai, there is a vast array of treatments to select from here. The Mandarin's spa has won many awards worldwide.

417 CHI SPA
AT: SHANGRI-LA

89 Soi Wat Suan Plu
Silom/Bang Rak ②
+66 (0)2 236 7777
www.shangri-la.com/
bangkok

Countless publications have chosen CHI as one of the best spas in the world. The most unique treatment here involves the use of hot stones to relax the body, followed by a body scrub in which organic black jasmine rice is blended with honey and herbs to get rid of dead and rough skin.

418 ELEMIS SPA
AT: ST. REGIS HOTEL

159 Rajadamri Road
Pathumwan ①
+66 (0)2 207 7779
www.elemisspabangkok.
com

This spa features a Rasul chamber, which is an ancient Arabian bathing ritual incorporating clay, heat, and steam to cleanse toxins. They also have a four-hour anti-ageing treatment with a lime and ginger salt glow, body sculpting therapy, and deep tissue massage.

419 SO SPA
AT: SOFITEL SO

2 North Sathorn Road
Sathorn ⑥
+66 (0)2 624 0000
www.so-sofitel-bangkok.
com/wellness/sospa

The elegant SO Spa has a Turkish *hamman*, a bath where you lay on hot marble to heat up, then get washed, scrubbed, and cleansed from head to toe. Amongst the array of exotic treatments here, you can go for a cucumber and honey facial, a Moroccan *beldi* black soap scrub, a Javanese spice scrub, or a pink Himalayan salt wrap.

420 KEMPINSKI THE SPA
AT: SIAM KEMPINSKI HOTEL

991/9 Rama I Road
Pathumwan ①
+66 (0)2 162 9000
www.kempinski.com/
en/bangkok/siam-hotel/
luxury-spa

Voted the World's Best Spa in 2015 at the Spa and Wellness Awards in London. You can choose from an array of season-focused treatment options here. 'Winter' treatments are warm and energising, while 'Summer' ones are cool and refreshing. They do hot stone, herbal compress, and traditional Thai massage only as well.

The 5
BEST-VALUE SPAS

---

421 THE TOUCH

11/2 Ruam Ruedee
Pathumwan ⑦
+66 (0)2 651 5722
www.thetouch1.com

There are few spas in Bangkok where you can get a body scrub combined with a Thai massage for less than 1000 baht, but at The Touch it's a mere 890. Additionally, their one-hour foot, shoulder, and back massages go as low as 350 baht.

422 HEALTH LAND

55/5 Sukhumvit Soi 21
(Asoke)
Sukhumvit ⑦
+66 (0)2 261 1110
www.healthlandspa.com

Sit in a wooden steam chamber filled with medicated herbs, detoxing with an Ayurvedic steam bath or go for a Shiro Dhara Ayurvedic warm oil treatment, where oil is slowly dripped and massaged on your forehead. From Ayurvedic to Thai herbal, they do it all here. They are very popular amongst locals with prices not much higher than streetside cheapies.

423 ASIA HERB ASSOCIATION

50/6 Sukhumvit Soi 24
Sukhumvit ⑦
+66 (0)2 261 7401
www.asiaherb
association.com

Asia Herb Association specialises in organic herbal compresses, with herbs coming from their own farm in Khao Yai. A great massage here goes for only 500 baht, and they are one of the only late night spas in town, so you can get a rubdown at midnight if you choose so.

424 DIVANA NURTURE SPA

71 Sukhumvit Soi 11
Sukhumvit ⑦
+66 (0)2 651 2916
www.divanaspa.com

Divana is at the top of the list if you want long, pampering great-value spa journeys. Their signature treatment lasts over four hours and includes foot baths, hot herbal compresses, detox body scrubs, facial, and even a Thai rice wine body soak, along with their acclaimed acupressure and top-notch Thai massage techniques.

425 RUEN NUAD

42 Convent Road
Silom ②
+66 (0)2 632 2662

Ruen Nuad offers no-frills traditional Thai massage at its best. No swanky signature treatments with exotic creams or oils to be found here, just a choice of Thai massage, oil massage, or foot massage at prices that will leave plenty of change left over for cocktails afterwards.

424 DIVANA NURTURE SPA

5 WELLNESS ALTERNATIVES
to keep in mind

---

426 MOWAAN
9 Soi Tessa, Bamrung
Muang Road
Rattanakosin Island ③
+66 (0)2 221 8070
www.mowaan.com

This is a herbal medicine clinic in which the owner continues her great-grandfather's tradition of *ya hom*, herbal treatments that are comprised of fragrant herbs used to cure fever, constipation, and other maladies. The shop has been open since 1924 and is a museum as well as a clinic.

427 HUA CHIEW ACUPUNCTURE CLINIC
665 Bamrung Muang
Road
Rattanakosin Island ③
+66 (0)2 223 1351
www.hc-hospital.com

Acupuncture is a great alternative remedy to help with chronic pain or other general body woes. This Chinese hospital has an acupuncture therapist training section; you see a doctor, and she brings her interns in to watch her heated-needle treatments. As a training centre, it's much cheaper than other places, but it is safe and well-run.

428 I.SAWAN RESIDENTIAL SPA & CLUB
AT: GRAND HYATT ERAWAN
494 Rajadamri Road
Pathumwan ①
+66 (0)2 254 1234
www. bangkok.grand.
hyatt.com

Where else can you do a 6-hour spa treatment and follow it up with circuit training or a yoga workout in a greenhouse gym and a relax session in a free-form swimming pool? You can also get a salon treatment as part of this all in one wellness escape.

429 BANGKOK FLOAT CENTER
AT: SHOW DC ENTERTAINMENT
MALL, 4TH FLOOR
99/6-9 Rim Khlong
Bangkapi Road
Northern Bangkok ⑪
+66 (0)98 628 9599
www.bangkok
floatcenter.com

Floatation tanks are soundproof chambers that are filled with body temperature epsom salt water, allowing the user to float effortlessly and peacefully without disturbance, giving a meditative and relaxing experience. This is Bangkok's only floatation centre and there is a choice of small pods or slightly larger tanks to float in.

430 YUNOMORI ONSEN
AT: A-SQUARE
120/5 Sukhumvit Soi 26
Sukhumvit ⑦
+66 (0)2 259 5778
www.yunomorionsen.
com/2015/bangkok

Yunomori caters to the needs of *onsen* hot spring lovers. The owners here have transported 3000 litres of hot spring water from a natural spring in southern Thailand, and there is a range of different temperature pools to choose from, along with a whirlpool bath that has a carbonated soda water generator, which mixes soda and water and promotes blood circulation and rejuvenation.

430 YUNOMORI ONSEN

5 great places to get a
TRADITIONAL
THAI MASSAGE

---

431 **WAT PHO THAI TRADITIONAL MASSAGE SCHOOL**
392/33-34 Maharaj Road
Rattanakosin Island ③
+66 (0)2 622 3551
www.watpomassage.com

While tourists flock here to see the giant Buddha in the temple, Wat Pho is just as renowned for its massage school, in operation since 1962, and offering both massage courses and treatments. You can have the advanced students massage you in an open-air pavilion for a pittance, in what are heavenly surroundings.

432 **TRADITIONAL THAI MEDICINE RESEARCH INSTITUTE**
693 Bamrungmuang Road
Dusit ⑩
+66 (0)2 224 3261
www.tmri.dtam.moph.go.th

Thai traditional medicine is similar to Chinese and Indian medicine in that it is holistic, seeking to treat the cause of an ailment as opposed to the symptoms. At this old-school clinic you can have treatments with hot herbal compresses and herbal steam baths, followed by traditional massage.

433 **PERCEPTION BLIND MASSAGE**
Sathorn Soi 8
Sathorn ⑥
+66 (0)82 222 5936
www.perception
blindmassage.com

The blind rely on touch, so it's not surprising that Perception consistently gets touted for giving some of the best massages in town. The masseurs and masseuses here are all blind or visually impaired, and most have been trained in the art of touch for many years.

434 MYTH

28/3 Soi Ruamrudee
Pathumwan ⑦
+66 (0)2 651 5600
www.siamyth.com

A signature organic oil massage with herbal compresses weighs in at 1250 baht for 80 minutes here, and the suave townhouse setting with a rooftop bar rivals high end hotel rubdown spots, making it great value for some upmarket pampering at common-folk prices.

435 URBAN RETREAT

348/1 Sukhumvit (at
Asok intersection)
Sukhumvit ⑦
+66 (0)2 229 4701
www.urbanretreatspa.net

With a wide menu of traditional massages, body masks and scrubs, and even 'four hands' rubdowns, it's hard to choose here, and not only is the spa menu extensive, the prices are good for a place that uses high quality oils and gives attentive service. Massages start at 500 baht an hour, and you can get 2-hour package promotions daily.

432 TRADITIONAL THAI MEDICINE RESEARCH INSTITUTE

The 5 best
SALONS

---

436 MARK THAWIN ULTIMATE HAIR SOLUTION
AT: TOWN IN TOWN
330 Si Vara Soi 94
Northern Bangkok ⑪
+66 (0)2 934 7776

Thawin is a flamboyant Thai stylist, probably the best known amongst the celebrity and fashion crowd, and he's done many a hairstyle of those gracing the catwalks. It's worth the trip to Northern Bangkok to check out his stylist school and pampering salon, and while prices are high, getting what you pay for is guaranteed here.

437 ZENRED HAIR SALON
AT: MONOPOLY PARK
59/27 Industrial Ring Road
Southern Bangkok ⑬
+66 (0)83 600 6176
www.zenredsalon bangkok.com

Hair extensions, colouring, Brazilian keratin treatments, and straightening, Zenred pretty much does it all. They are also the most tourist-friendly shop to be found in Bangkok, taking pride in their English-speaking services and fact that they've served expats and visitors for over 25 years. At 500 baht for a superior cut, they are half the price of some of the more glitzy salons.

438 HIVE HAIR & NAIL
AT: THE PORTICO LIFESTYLE
MALL, 4TH FLOOR

31 Soi Langsuan
Pathumwan ①
+66 (0)2 020 0956

Considering that a good number of Thai celebrities get their hair cut here, you're most likely in excellent company. The salon is named after the large number of beehive-shaped chandeliers that owner Krit Jirakiatwattana has decorated his two branches with. They specialise in vintage men's barbering, ladies' hairdressing, and manicures and pedicures.

439 TRUEFITT AND HILL
AT: CENTRAL EMBASSY,
4TH FLOOR

1031 Ploenchit Road
Pathumwan ①
+66 (0)98 363 6146
www.truefittandhill
thailand.com

England's oldest barber (dating back to 1805) has expanded to Asia, and men's grooming doesn't get any finer than this. The shop resembles a gentlemen's club, with comfy leather barber chairs, and you can get creative beard and hair designs or settle in for a shave using traditional brushes and foams.

440 TONI & GUY
AT: THE ESPLANADE,
2ND FLOOR

99 Ratchadapisek Road
Northern Bangkok ⑪
+66 (0)2 660 9212
www.toniandguy.com/
salon/bangkok

The sponsor of London Fashion Week, Toni & Guy is now a renowned international name, doing innovative hair styling for men and women. London-trained stylists are frequented by the celebrity and VIP crowd here, and yet prices remain on par with the competitors'.

5 places for FITNESS AND ALTERNATIVE WORKOUTS

---

441 **ABSOLUTE YOGA**
AT: AMARIN PLAZA,
11TH FLOOR
496-502 Ploenchit Road
Pathumwan ①
+66 (0)2 252 4400
www.absoluteyou.com

From hot to Hatha or Vinyasa yoga, Absolute has a class for you. They have seven branches around town, have Pilates, bike spinning, and core blast classes in addition to the yoga, and they have a very well-trained fleet of English speaking instructors. They have ongoing classes throughout the day and evening, plus drop-in rates and longer promotions.

442 **VIRGIN ACTIVE**
AT: EMQUARTIER, 4TH FLOOR
689 Sukhumvit Road
Sukhumvit ⑦
+66 (0)2 770 9797
www.virginactive.co.th

This is Bangkok's most pampering club, so ritzy that you might spend more time in the Himalayan salt steam or ice room than on the climbing wall or in the swimming pool. They even have a high-altitude training room here, which simulates life at 3000 metres, just in case you are training for the Mexico City marathon or an Everest expedition.

443 PHYSIQUE 57

AT: ERAWAN BANGKOK
BUILDING
494 Ploenchit Road
Pathumwan ①
+66 (0)2 652 1703
www.physique57
bangkok.com

This fancy fitness club started in Manhattan, spread to the Hamptons and Beverly Hills, and now is in Bangkok. Classes focus on ballet barre-based workouts that sculpt lean muscles in 30- or 57-minute sessions. You can do drop-ins here, and join the bevy of beautiful people dancing to the music. Instruction is in English.

444 SURF SET

AT: PIMAN 49, 5TH FLOOR
46/4 Sukhumvit Soi 49
Sukhumvit ⑦
+66 (0)2 662 4566
www.surfsetthailand.com

For those who want to surf (but are scared of waves and sharks), Surf Set provides a chance to go indoor surfing. A former U.S. hockey player invented this, and doing yoga poses on a moving automated board has become a big fad due to the fun factor involved, not to mention you get in shape as well.

445 THE RACQUET CLUB

8 Sukhumvit Soi 49/9
Sukhumvit ⑦
+66 (0)2 119 7200
www.rqclub.com

With 2 swimming pools, 7 rooftop tennis courts, squash and badminton, a fitness centre, and an 80-route climbing wall, this is Bangkok's one-stop shop for the workout lover. They even have a free shuttle from the Skytrain. Come in here to do a trial and you might end up in Bangkok a lot longer than planned.

SANGKHLABURI

25 ACTIVITIES
FOR WEEKENDS

The 5 nearest
BEACHES

---

446 KO SAMET
Rayong District
Chonburi Province

Ko Samet is a real island escape. The beaches are lovely, especially the further south you head, and the one west coast beach offers magnificent sunsets, along with more upscale accommodation than the east side. It's packed on weekends but gloriously empty during the week.

447 CHA AM
Phetchaburi Province

Cha Am plays second fiddle to Hua Hin, so much that many resorts here label themselves Cha Am-Hua Hin in the hopes of drawing traffic. It's really sleepy here during the week. While the sand isn't blindingly white, it's an easy and affordable Bangkok escape.

448 HUA HIN
Hua Hin
Prachuap Khiri Khan
Province

This was Thailand's first beach tourism resort, initially because the rail line ran through here, and it later became the residence out of Bangkok for the king and queen. The beaches are pleasant enough, and it is one of the few places to go horseback riding on the beach.

449 THAM PANG BEACH, KO SI CHANG

Ko Si Chang Island
Chonburi Province

Ko Si Chang is a small island in the Bight of Bangkok, mostly noted for its temples and as a city escape that sees few foreign tourists. It does have this one lovely small beach on its west coast though, which has a resort to stay at, plus better ones up on the cliffs above.

450 KO LARN

Na Kleua
Chonburi Province

While Pattaya is far more noted for its nefarious nightlife and fairly abysmal beaches, the offshore island of Ko Larn will have you thinking you are somewhere far south in the Andaman. Emerald bays and white sand beaches are the norm, and if you decide to stay overnight, you'll have the place almost all to yourself, as most visitors just come over on daytrips from Pattaya.

450 **KO LARN**

The 5 best
OUTDOOR ESCAPES

---

451 KHAO SAM ROI YOT NATIONAL PARK

Kuiburi District
Prachuap Khiri Khan
Province
+66 (0)89 782 6002
*www.thainationalparks.
com/khao-sam-roi-yot-
national-park*

Forty minutes south of Hua Hin you'll find Sam Roi Yot (meaning '300 hills' in Thai), a gem of a national park that features inland hiking trails, several nice beaches, thousands of migrating birds during the winter season, and a fantastic magical royal throne room inside a collapsed sinkhole cave.

452 ERAWAN NATIONAL PARK

Tha Kradan
Kanchanaburi Province
+66 (0)34 574 222
*www.thainationalparks.
com/erawan-national-park*

The highlight of Erawan is a several kilometre stretch of multi-tiered waterfalls with cascading pools, incredibly photogenic as well as suitable for swimming. There are seven falls to visit on the way up through the park, with few visitors actually reaching the top tier.

453 KAENG KRACHAN NATIONAL PARK

Petchaburi Province
+66 (0)32 459 293
*www.thainationalparks.
com/kaeng-krachan-
national-park*

This is Thailand's largest national park, and it features trekking to mountain peaks with seas of mist in the valley, abundant wildlife from wild boar and elephant to dusky langurs, along with pristine waterfalls and not too many tourists.

454 KHAO LOM MUAK

Ko Lak
Prachuap Khiri Khan
Province

This pointed peak sits at the end of a beautiful beach in Prachuap Khiri Khan, and is controlled by the Thai Air Force. You sign in at the gate to access the beach area, then sign in again for the climb, which gives gorgeous views of the entire coastline. Additionally, there are dusky langur monkeys in the forest at the bottom.

455 KHAO YAI NATIONAL PARK

Hin Tung
Nakhon Nayok Province
+66 (0)86 092 6529
www.thainationalparks. com/khao-yai-national- park

Khao Yai was Thailand's first national park, and is now a UNESCO World Heritage Site. The large park is home to 3000 plant species and 300 different birds, as well as abundant wildlife – like Asian elephant herds. You can hike, go to wildlife observation towers, and visit spectacular waterfalls.

451 KHAO SAM ROI YOT NATIONAL PARK

454 KHAO LOM MUAK

5 must-see
ATTRACTIONS

---

456 WAT BANG KHUN
Rural Road 4013
Samut Songkhram
Province

More reminiscent of something you might find in Angkor Wat, this temple is more commonly referred to as 'the temple in the tree', as it is completely engulfed by the roots of a banyan tree. There is a golden Buddha image inside, illuminated by candles, but the view from the outside is most impressive.

457 MAE KHLONG TRAIN MARKET
Soi Kasem Sukhum
Mae Klong
Samut Songkhram
Province
+66 (0)98 425 2451

Also known as the umbrella market, this unique market is perched right on the train tracks. When the four local trains per day come through here, the vendors must fold up their umbrellas while the train comes through, with just millimetres to spare between the market and the train.

458 AYUTTHAYA
Pratuchai
Phra Nakhon Sri
Ayutthaya Province

Thailand's ancient capital should be on every visitor's day trip list. Easily reached by train, the UNESCO World Heritage site and historical park is full of beautiful old ruins, many in great shape, with stone towers and large temples. Touring them by bicycle and boat is a popular way to go.

459 **KANCHANABURI**
Kanchanaburi Province

Site of the film *The Bridge on the River Kwai*, you'll find the famous Railway Bridge here, along with other spots that commemorate the infamous Death Railway run by the Japanese during World War II. There are several war and railway museums to visit, as well as the somber POW (prisoners of war) War Cemetery.

460 **PHRAYA NAKHON CAVE**
AT: KHAO SAM ROI YOT NP
Kuiburi District
Prachuap Khiri Khan
Province
+66 (0)89 782 6002
www.thainationalparks.com/khao-sam-roi-yot-national-park

This amazing attraction features a throne constructed for King Rama V, who visited the cave in 1890. The throne is placed inside a large cavern made up of two sinkhole caves whose roofs have collapsed. In the early morning, light filters in from the opening and illuminates the golden throne. It's the most photographed cave in Thailand.

460 PHRAYA NAKHON CAVE

The 5 best
WATER-BASED
activities

---

461 **BANG TABUN WHALE WATCHING**
Ban Laem District
Petchaburi Province
+66 (0)99 292 2666
www.wildencounter
thailand.com

Few tourists coming to Thailand would think that they'd be going whale watching here, but surprisingly, the Gulf of Thailand near to Bangkok offers great opportunities to see schools of Bryde's whales, as well as the endangered Irrawaddy dolphin. Wild Encounter Thailand offers trips every weekend from May to December.

462 **AMPHAWA FLOATING MARKET**
Amphawa District
Samut Songkhram Province
www.amphawatoday.com

Far more authentic than the nearby Damnoen Saduak, the Amphawa floating market is aimed at Bangkok Thais wanting to enjoy a timeless Thai tradition. Set along the Amphawa canal, the market runs Friday through Sunday. The biggest draw are the seafood boats, where giant prawns and crab dishes are hawked for a fraction of the price you'd pay in the city.

463 FISHING
AT: NEW BUNGSAMRAN LAKE
Sala Daeng 9, Bang Nam
Priao, Chachoengsao
Eastern Bangkok
+66 (0)38 090 979
www.newbungsamran.com

If you are after catching the biggest fish you've ever seen in your life, you'll love Bungsamran, as they stock this catch and release lake with Giant Mekong Catfish and Siamese Carp which can weigh up to 100 kilos. Casual fishermen can hire guides, rent rods, and learn what it takes to reel in a monster!

464 SAILING
AT: ROYAL VARUNA YACHT
CLUB
286 Moo 12 Phatumnak
Road, Nongprue
Chonburi Province
+66 (0)38 250 116
www.varuna.org

Most people don't associate the Pattaya area with sailing, but there are some excellent conditions here, especially during the cool winter season, to learn to navigate your own yacht. You can take 2-day Yachting Association-accredited courses here and then rent sailboats. The Yacht Club has their own private beach, a swimming pool, and even a place to stay at their well-run facility not too far from Pattaya.

465 KITE SURFING IN CHA AM
289/3 Phetkasem Road,
Cha Am Soi 53
Tassanee Beach, Amphoe
Hua Hin
Petchaburi Province
+66 (0)98 549 8993
www.17knots
kitesurfcenter.com

Cha Am is windy the year round, one reason why the beach town hosts an annual kite festival. You can do a 9-hour kite surfing course here which will get you ready to go out and handle the waves, and the kite surfing school here is not only a learning centre, but also a relaxed hangout with a great community vibe.

5 great
HIDDEN ESCAPES

---

466 **BAN KRUT**

**Bang Saphan District
Prachuap Khiri Khan
Province**

If you want to experience Thai island life and local hospitality the way it was decades ago, make a beeline for Ban Krut. This sleepy beach town is on the train line south, so it is easy to access from Bangkok. The white sand beaches are as good as Samui, yet with a fraction of the people, costs, or hassles.

467 **SAMUT SAKHON SALT FARMS**

Southwest of Bangkok

If you are in Thailand during the dry season (January to May), it's worth stopping off at the triangular white mounds you will see gleaming off to the sides of the Samut Sakhon road. When it gets really hot, water evaporates and they make salt here, with the area looking like a miniature version of Bolivia's famed salt flats.

468 **PRANBURI**

**Prachuap Khiri Khan
Province**

Pranburi is what Hua Hin was 50 years ago. Though being less than 40 minutes by car from Hua Hin, it is kilometres removed, with just a small selection of elegant resorts nestled against the quiet beaches. You can go hiking here, or just enjoy fresh seafood on the beach.

469 SAI YOK

Sai Yok District
Kanchanaburi Province
+66 (0)86 700 7442
*www.thainationalparks.
com/sai-yok-national-park*

Between Kanchanaburi and Sangkhlaburi you'll find this national park, which has one section on the north side of the highway with a small waterfall, and another just up the road on the south. Just head to the second, where you will find floating raft-house bungalows along the river that ooze charm and atmosphere. This is a great spot to spend a night, watching fireflies and lazing on the water.

470 SANGKHLABURI

Sangkhlaburi Province

Located near the Myanmar border, Sangkhlaburi has a frontier feel. The town sits on a large former reservoir-lake which covers a sunken city, of which a former temple can be visited by boat during the dry season, as it pokes up out of the water. There is also one of the world's longest wooden footbridges here.

469 SAI YOK

MAHANAKHON TOWER

30 RANDOM FACTS AND URBAN DETAILS

5
MOVIES
set in Bangkok

471 GOOD MORNING VIETNAM

One of the best films portraying life in Southeast Asia. This was also one of Robin Williams' most defining roles, playing a radio DJ during the Vietnam War. While the film portrays life in Saigon, Bangkok was actually the setting used for the city scenes. His *object d'amour* in the film was also a noted Thai actress: Jintara Sukapat.

472 THE HANGOVER II

The raunchy U.S. comedy shot its sequel to the Las Vegas party epic in Bangkok, along with Krabi down south. The rooftop scenes were shot at the Sky Bar in the Lebua State Tower, and spawned the creation of the bar's signature drink, the Hangovertini.

473 BANGKOK DANGEROUS

This crime thriller starring Nicholas Cage was shot on location in Bangkok. An interesting note about the film was that the filming was delayed due to the political coup d'état that occurred while the movie was being made.

474 BRIDGET JONES: THE EDGE OF REASON

The sequel to the popular romantic comedy *Bridget Jones's Diary* was filmed both in Phuket and Phang Nga Bay as well as in Bangkok, and starred Hugh Grant, Rene Zellweger, and Colin Firth. Most of the Bangkok scenes were shot around the Red Light nightlife area of Soi Cowboy, which has become a popular shooting area for films wanting an infamous and iconic Bangkok landmark.

475 THE MAN WITH THE GOLDEN GUN

The James Bond classic with Roger Moore was shot in Bangkok as well as down on the islands around Phang Nga Bay. The film's epic car chase scene was done in Bangkok, as was the muay thai boxing match, which was filmed at Ratchadamnoen Boxing Stadium.

472 THE HANGOVER II - SKY BAR

5
BOOKS TO READ
set in Bangkok

---

476 **BANGKOK 8**
BY JOHN BURDETT

Bangkok-based John Burdett writes fictional crime novels set in Bangkok's sleazier quarters. This is his most famous of a series, and although it might be easy to dismiss it as pulp fiction, it actually gives great insight into Thai culture, Buddhism, and the sex trade, as well as being a well-written crime thriller.

477 **BANGKOK DAYS**
BY LAWRENCE OSBORNE

New York based travel writer Lawrence Osborne delivers one of the best written novels on Bangkok's blend of east and west, glamour and sleaze, and an insight to the bowels of the city. His nighttime explorations bring the city alive. *The New York Times* called the book 'wickedly enjoyable'.

478 THE DAMAGE DONE
BY WARREN FELLOWS

Many books have been written about the notorious Bangkok prisons (dubbed the Bangkok Hilton), but this one is the best, detailing Warren Fellows' descent into hell after he was caught and convicted of smuggling heroin and sentenced to 12 years in Bangkok jails.

479 THE WINDUP GIRL
BY PAOLO BACIGALUPI

Author Paolo Bacigalupi won the Sturgeon Award as well as being a finalist for the National Book of the Year. This fascinating look at Bangkok takes place in an apocalyptic future without oil, where rising sea levels and out-of-control mutation rule the roost. The book won four different national awards and is a captivating sci-fi read.

480 COCKROACHES
BY JO NESBØ

This number one The New York Times Best Seller is one of a series of detective novels written by Jo Nesbø, a Norwegian writer, musician, and economist, that follow the misadventures of detective Harry Hole. In this exciting thriller, he comes to Bangkok to discover why the Norwegian ambassador has been found dead in a Bangkok brothel.

5

QUIRKY FACTS

about Bangkok life and culture

---

481 NAME

The real name of Bangkok in Thai is 'Krungthepmahanakhon Amonrattanakosin Mahintharayutthaya Mahadilokphop Noppharatratchathaniburirom Udomratchaniwetmahasathan Amonphimanawatansathit Sakkathattiyawitsanukamprasit', making it the longest name of any capital city in the world.

482 TALLEST BUILDING

Until 2016, the tallest building in Bangkok was the Baiyoke Tower II, measuring up at 309 metres. It has since been surpassed by the MahaNakhon Tower, which at 314 metres is the 88th tallest building in the world. Plans are afoot to build the Rama IX Super Tower, which at 615 metres will nearly double the height of the MahaNakhon.

483 SINKING BANGKOK

Bangkok is sinking at a rate of over two centimetres per year. Scientists estimate that it could be underwater in as little as fifteen years from now, so better come visit it soon! Built over canals and swamp, and with over 4000 high-floor buildings pressing down on it, combined with rising global sea levels, reports say that the city will most surely be completely submerged by the year 2100.

484 LARGEST BUDDHA

The largest gold Buddha statue in the world can be found in Bangkok. The sitting Buddha image that is housed in Wat Traimit in Chinatown is made entirely of 18 karat gold and weighs five and a half tons (5500 kilos). It is worth over 250 million euros! The statue is from ancient Ayutthaya, although the massive gold was not found until after the statue (covered in plaster at the time) was dropped after being moved to Bangkok.

485 COINS

Bangkok's most famous temples are all on the back of Thai coins. Wat Arun is on the 10 baht piece, Wat Benjamabophit is on the 5 baht coin, Wat Saket on the 2 baht, and Wat Phra Kaew on the 1 baht.

5 essential Bangkok
WEBSITES

486 THAI VISA

www.thaivisa.com

Whether you are considering moving to Thailand, want to know where you can find a specific battery or want recommendations for sushi, Thai Visa covers it all, with an open public forum, news page, and all sorts of listings relating to everything Thai. It's one of the top go-to websites for information for expatriates, with visitors using it almost as much.

487 EATING THAI FOOD

www.eatingthaifood.com

Thai food blogger Mark Wiens has become legendary, with a rabid following of his food website and youtube channel, as he good-humoredly eats his way around the country. His knowledge of Thai food is unrivalled, and he is a wealth of information on authentic Thai cuisine.

488 BK MAGAZINE
www.bk.asia-city.com

BK Magazine is Bangkok's only English-language weekly, and has become an excellent source for learning about new restaurant and bar openings, as well as finding out about art, music, and other cultural offerings. In addition to the weekly copy, available widely at coffee shops and bars, they also do daily reviews on their website.

489 BANGKOK.COM
www.bangkok.com

Another all-encompassing website on just about every Thai attraction, restaurant, bar, and other offering that a visitor to Bangkok might want. While the reviews often only cover the most common or trendy spots, it is a useful site if you want to get a decent selection of top places to visit.

490 RICHARD BARROW
www.richardbarrow.com

Blogger Richard Barrow has lived in and has been exploring Thailand for over twenty years. He was one of the country's first travel bloggers in the 1990s. He now does blogging and social media full time, has connections with Thai Tourism and the tourist industry, and is a fantastic source of off-the-beaten-path info and advice.

5 famous
THAIS

491 KING BHUMIBOL ADULYADEJ

Recently passed away (October 2016), King Bhumibol was the world's longest reigning monarch, and still is a revered deity-like figure in Thai society. He brought Thailand into the modern age, bringing revolutionary techniques like artificial rainmaking, soil improvement, and a high quality vegetable Royal Project. He was also an accomplished jazz saxophonist, sailor, and photographer, amongst other talents.

492 TONY JAA

A martial arts expert and stuntman, as well as actor and director, Japanon Yeerum, better known as Tony Jaa, is Thailand's best-known international actor, having starred in *Tom Yum Goong*, *Furious 7* and *Ong-Bak*, all styled after the films of his heroes – Bruce Lee and Jackie Chan. Jaa studied martial arts at a temple school and then college before being noticed by the film industry when he acted as a stunt double in *Mortal Combat*.

493 SEK LOSO

Sek Sukpimai was a poor kid from Thailand's impoverished northeast who talked his way onstage with his guitar in a club, and the rest is history. He is one of Thailand's most successful musicians, selling almost a dozen rock albums that have gone platinum, and has played international festivals like Glastonbury and South by Southwest. His nickname comes from a play on hi-so, high society, and reflects his own humble background.

494 THAKSIN SHINAWATRA

Controversial Thaksin Shinawatra was Thailand's former prime minister, famed for his populist policies and seen as a champion of the poor and leader of the Red Shirt political party. However, he was also seen as power hungry, and caught in embezzlement schemes. He was deposed of in a military coup and has been in self-imposed exile ever since.

495 TATA YOUNG

Tata Young is a Thai singer, born to a Thai mother and an American father, famed for her single *Dhoom Dhoom*, which sold almost one million copies in India after it was used for a Bollywood movie soundtrack. Young has made nine albums, and *Elle Magazine* named her as one of Thailand's 10 most influential people.

5

DATES OF NOTE

in Thai history

496 **APRIL 21, 1782**

The beginning of the Chakri Dynasty and the date that Bangkok became a capital city. General Chao Phraya Chakri was named King Ramathibodi (also known as Rama I) on April 6. Two weeks later, he chose a patch of ground next to the Chao Phraya River to erect a city pillar, declaring Bangkok as the new capital of Siam.

497 **JUNE 24, 1932**

The Siamese Revolution. Thailand was close to bankruptcy during the global Great Depression, much of it blamed on the archaic and corrupt government. A group of seven Thai student intellectuals led a People's Party movement for change. This eventually resulted in a bloodless coup, followed by the government changing from an absolute monarchy to a constitutional monarchy.

498 **OCTOBER 14, 1973**

Known as the 'day of great sorrow' in Thai, this major event resulted in the subsequent removal of the military dictatorship and is seen as a 'freedom day' by most Thais. That day, 77 people were killed, the majority of them students from Thammasat University who had taken to the streets and demanded that the military step down from politics.

499 **APRIL 10, 2010**

This polarising day in Thai history was the culmination of UDD – United Front of Democracy Against Dictatorship, also known as the 'red shirts' – supporters demanding early elections from a government backed by 'yellow shirt' royalist supporters. Peaceful sit-ins began to turn violent, and eventually the military was called in. 24 people were shot on April 10, with many more casualties happening again in the second week of May.

500 **OCTOBER 13, 2016**

Thai king Bhumibol Adulyadej, the longest reigning living monarch in the world, passed away after a 70-year reign. The 9th Thai king Adulyadej was seen as a god-like figure, and widely adored throughout the country. He led Thailand into the modern era, opened Siam to the west, and was famed for undertaking very successful social and economic rural agricultural development projects which still exist today.

INDEX